# What I Wish
## I Had Known
### About Becoming a
# Teenager

# What I Wish I Had Known About Becoming a Teenager

Wisdom and
Advice from
Teens in
High School

Saint Mary's Press®

Genuine recycled paper with 10% post-consumer waste. 5105500

The publishing team included Maura Thompson Hagarty, development editor; Lorraine Kilmartin, reviewer; Mary Koehler, permissions editor; Banana Stock / Media Bakery, cover image; prepress and manufacturing coordinated by the production departments of Saint Mary's Press.

Printed in the United States of America

ISBN 978-0-88489-662-3

Library of Congress Cataloging-in-Publication Data

What I wish I had known about becoming a teenager : wisdom and advice from teens in high school / edited by Maura Thompson Hagarty.
     p. cm.
ISBN 978-0-88489-662-3 (pbk.)
     1. Catholic teenagers—Religious life. 2. Teenagers—Conduct of life. 3. Adolescence. I. Hagarty, Maura Thompson.
BX2355.W48 2007
646.700835—dc22

2006034197

# Contents

# Preface

Whether you are excited or apprehensive about the teenage years, there is something in this book is for you. It is a collection of writings by high school students from across the United States. The writers explore lots of topics relevant to teenage life today: discovering who you are, being smart about technology, making friends, living your faith, staying out of harm's way, relating to parents and siblings, dealing with peer pressure, putting media messages in perspective, and being successful at school. The teens tell stories about their experiences, share insights about what they have learned, and offer great advice for younger teens and preteens.

## Thanks

Almost six hundred teenagers responded to Saint Mary's Press's invitation to submit writings for consideration in this book. We are thankful for each and every one and regret that only a fraction could be included. Thanks also to all the high school teachers and parish leaders who encouraged their students and teenage parishioners to reflect on their experiences and put their wisdom and advice in writing for the sake of other young people.

Maura Thompson Hagarty, editor

# Being a Teen

**The best advice** that I can give about the transition from childhood to adolescence is not to worry. Preteens shouldn't stress over the significant physical, intellectual, and emotional changes that will come as they become teenagers. Remember that each and every adolescent is going through these same changes, no matter how bizarre they may seem. The transition from childhood to adolescence is often a rocky one. Expect to make mistakes from time to time. Don't worry about making errors. Mistakes are a person's greatest teacher. Enjoy becoming a teenager, because it only happens once.

Michael J. Sanders

## A Whole New World

Although the teenage years are often presented as angst-ridden and overly emotional by the media, the reality is that these years are some of the best in our lives. As teenagers, we have a difficult but rewarding balance between freedom and responsibility. We can see, feel, and do new things. Our relationships with others have the ability to grow deeper and more mature. A whole new world is opened before us.

Dane Davis

## Managing Time

The biggest challenge teenagers face is trying to balance everything that is going on in their lives. It gets so complicated to play sports, hang out with friends, keep a boyfriend or girlfriend, cram for that huge history exam, find a ride to get to work on time, and find time to eat "healthy" (how often does that happen?). Then we have to talk about our day with our parents, after checking out colleges online. It gets so frustrating and overwhelming that you just want to dig a hole and hide in it forever. The thing most teenagers, including myself, need to work on is time management. Once there's a set schedule, it will take that enormous boulder that's weighing you down off your shoulders, and you will even have time to watch television, or even hit up the mall. There will be more than one stressful week in your teenage years, do not get me wrong, but there are ways to deal with this.

The worst thing anyone can do is bottle everything up and have no one to cry and scream with. If the people you want to tell aren't listening to you fully, guidance counselors are an amazing help. Don't be shy when you need to talk about a problem. Hiding it makes every situation worse. There is somebody, somewhere that has that same problem. People will understand; there is no need for you to be against the world.

So my young friends, time management will save you, but not as much as a good listener will. It's better to have one true friend that will help you through anything, and put you before the world, than if you had one hundred acquaintances just to party with and sit with at the lunch table. Being a teenager can be the best part of your life one week and then the next week, the worst part of your life. But it's you who can control the ups and downs.

Mary Beth Hoagland

## Five Things to Remember When Beginning the Teen Years

1. The relationships that you have before your teen years will change. Everyone's do.

2. Your outlook on life, religion, politics, and many other aspects of society will change, and they must. You need to allow yourself to become the person that God has chosen you to be.

3. Be lenient with those around your age. They are also changing and learning. Don't put them down. Be supportive and allow them to grow.

4. Understand that your friends do not always know what is right for you, no matter how smart they seem or how good their idea sounds.

5. In your teenage years you hear the phrase "be yourself" quite often, but you don't know who you are yet. The better way to say it is, "Be who you want to be." That doesn't mean choose who you want to be every day . . . minute . . . second; it means find out what kind of person you want to be and be that.

Bri Boñer

**I am so happy** in my life right now. What happens can be ten times better than what you read in a book, see on a movie screen, or even dream.

Malinda Frevert

**Being a teenager** is such a complex experience that sometimes it's hard to explain. There are so many wonderful things that occur and so many challenges that come to pass. One of the best things about being a teenager is the friendships that develop during these years. I have such wonderful friends, and as you get older, your friendships become stronger because interests and worldviews change. Friends become your family, and they help you through the joys and challenges that life can bring to you. Friends help you to become who you truly are. Another great thing about being a teenager is the development of opinions and ideas. As you age, the way you see and understand the world changes, and being a teenager in high school allows discussion of such ideas and opinions. Life isn't comprised of television shows and toys anymore. The conversations that make up teenage life truly make it great.

Johi Koneval

**It is so great** to become a teenager. I personally think you will love it. Becoming a teenager is one of the best things that will ever happen to you.

Lenny Ragaglia

**The thing that** has surprised me the most about my teenage years is the utter realization of reality. In my preteens, I lived a "Candyland" life with sugarcoated truths and unrealistic intentions. I felt that having the title *teenager* would thrust me into adulthood and privy me to the late-night curfews, romantic nights, and most importantly, boys that were as tall as me. I looked toward those awkward teenage years as a time to reinvent myself.

Waking up on July 3, 2001, I half expected to have long blonde hair and a boy waiting at my breakfast table. Instead I got cheesy cards about growing up and thirteen punches from a friend. Although I had been expecting more, I didn't let my disappointment get the best of me.

I never found true love during my transitional years, nor the late-night endeavors, nor a non-height-deprived boy, but I started my journey into reality. Reality, with all its twists and surprises, is something I have learned to embrace and learn from. It's the things you don't expect that make you who you are and shape you. Surprises throughout my teens are what have helped me to continue to be the energetic and unpredictable person that I am.

Shaina Lee Miranda

## The Yellow Brick Road

I wish I had known becoming a teenager was like walking in Dorothy's ruby slippers down the Yellow Brick Road to see the wizard. You grow up in a nice house with your parents and a little dog like Toto. Everything seems to be perfect. Then one day a tornado hits: adolescence. Be careful what you wish for. You're not little anymore. You feel like you are all alone, dealing with your menstrual cycle, and your body is changing and developing. You used to see the world in black and white. All of a sudden, you feel as though you land in Oz, a world full of color. Everything is different. The munchkins are like all the boys you never noticed before, and you realize they now notice you. You just want to go back to Kansas, the security you once knew.

Glenda, your guardian angel, introduces herself and explains that adolescence will be like a long walk down the Yellow Brick Road. She gives you the ruby slippers and wishes you luck; it's a little scary, but exciting at the same time. Along the way, you meet your first guide, dressed as a scarecrow. He reminds you how lucky you are to have a brain, to always use your best judgment, to realize how intelligent you are, and to always choose the right road. Your second guide, the Tin Man, reminds you that your heart keeps you alive, to keep it healthy, and that you do survive a broken heart. Your third guide, the Lion, teaches you to muster up the courage to say no. He explains to you that fear is God's way of letting you know you're alive.

At every guide meeting, there is a visit from the Wicked Witch of the West, the devil, trying to spoil everything for you. She represents all the negativity, temptations, and emotions you have to deal with, including drugs, smoking, sex, alcohol, going along with the crowd, skipping school, and bullies. But Glenda always helps you and keeps you safe.

When you finally reach the Wizard, you know there is nothing in his bag for you. This becomes almost like an encounter with God. He acknowledges how proud of you he is and reminds you that you have traveled the road to maturity well, keeping your faith and achieving your goals. Glenda returns to explain how you had to take this journey to become who you are and to tell you that you always had the power and you always will. You say goodbye and thank all for their help and guidance.

Eventually you wake up and realize everything your parents said and warned you about growing up was right. But you'll never admit it.

Embrace and enjoy the journey. You'll have wonderful memories.

Erin Monahan

**The best thing** about the teenage years is receiving more independence. With this independence comes responsibility. During these years, it is important to choose your friends carefully. You do not want the kind of friends that are always looking for trouble.

Keeping God in your life during these teenage years is very important. You should pray to God to help you with teenage challenges. He will always guide you in the right direction. I stay close to God through prayer and by volunteering as an altar server. I have made some great friends through altar serving at my parish.

Another great thing about the teenage years is learning how to drive. Even though this is a very exciting time, it is also a very serious responsibility. High school is another great thing about being a teenager. You have the opportunity to meet different kids from all different schools. This helps you make new friends. I have made some great friends by joining bowling, an extracurricular activity after school.

Remember during your teenage years to choose your friends wisely, be responsible, and have fun. Always keep God in your life and your teenage years will be great!

**T**rust in God
**E**xciting
**E**xcellent
**N**ew experiences

**Y**ears to remember
**E**xtracurricular activities
**A**wesome friends
**R**esponsibility
**S**tay focused

Andrew Marotta

**You have to be dedicated** and focused in order to become a successful teenager, but you also have to have some fun. Try not to take life too seriously. Just think of worrying as a waste of your time!

Chris Sodano

## New Responsibilities

Before becoming a teenager, I wish I knew that I was going to have so much more responsibility and that I could not take it lightly. I also wish I knew that I couldn't be so childish and immature. Before becoming a teenager, everything was basically spoon-fed to me. Once I started getting bombarded with privileges, responsibilities, and choices, I was completely overwhelmed. But I realized that this was my initiation into adulthood, and I was going to have to start organizing my priorities. Looking back, I was really inexperienced in taking care of my responsibilities, such as deadlines, appointments, and chores. However, there was nothing I could do to escape these responsibilities. This was life, and I was going to have to learn to sort it all out on my own. Now I consider myself to be very independent; that independence came gradually, and eventually I learned to take care of myself. Sometimes I slip when it comes to childhood behaviors, but even with all the responsibilities, there is always time for play. You never get too old to play.

Megan Dae Hutton

## Moving On Up

Turning into a young adult
Can seem terrifying
Like the hardest thing to do
But if you think about it
You've been doing it for your
　　whole life
Adding the word *teen* to the
　　end of your age
Seems to fill us with anxiety
But with new times in your life
Comes new responsibility
New obstacles
Moving on up in your life
Being a young adult brings so
　　much excitement
Independence and the freedom
　　to make your own decisions
Nothing feels better than that
But in the shadows of the fun of
　　being a teen
Growing up ultimately and will
　　always
Bring new experiences to light
The first time you fall in love
The first time your heart gets
　　broken
The first group of friends you
　　realize are bad for you

The first time you turn them
　　down
The first time you succumb to
　　pressure
The first time you witness the
　　secret life of teens
Remember that everyone goes
　　through this
So talking about it isn't awk-
　　ward
Yes, even your parents have too
Step through the door into
　　adulthood
Without looking back
Look forward to all of your
　　"firsts"
And understand that facing
　　them
Requires fortitude
And the courage to decide
　　what is right
Moving on up like this
Is another chapter
That you can look back on in
　　your life
And say "I remember
　　when . . ."

Brianne M. Rogers

16

## When I Was Young

When I was young, I thought I knew all there is to know about
  growing up.
What to expect and how to deal with it.
Whom I was going to hang out with and whom I wasn't.
I am a teenager now, and I'm still trying to figure it out.
When I was young, I thought I knew exactly where I stood.
I would say no to anything that could harm me.
I would say no to anything that might break me.
I am a teenager now, and I'm caught in the middle.
When I was young, I thought I knew where I was going and who
  I wanted to be.
I would be rich and famous.
Everything would always go my way, and I'd be happy.
I am a teenager now, and I know that I have a lot to learn.
When I was young, I had no idea exactly how hard things would
  really be.
My advice to you is to stay who you are and hold on to your faith
  and morals.
My advice to you is to not let the ride control you, but you control
  the ride.
I am a teenager now, so I'm still on the ride, but I'm in control of
  what I do and say,
so my final advice to you is to please do the same.

Emily Geise

## Wake Up

"Wake up!" my mom yells down the stairs. I lurch forward, pulling my covers aside. It is the first day of seventh grade, and my adventure into junior high begins. I brush my teeth and comb my hair; I am ready to go. I have just spent the last seven years with the same friends and same teachers, and now I am being thrown into a school with double the students and only one friend from before. I open the door and head on in. I cannot seem to get rid of these butterflies in my stomach.

I take a deep breath. The butterflies still sit in the pit of my stomach like an anchor holding me down. I let the breath out. It is my eighth-grade graduation party. I walk into my first dance. I sit back against the wall; I am not really a dancer. If I do not ask someone to dance, my friend will do it for me. I give him the eye as I walk out to slow dance to what seems the longest song ever. As we move around in circles, I think to myself how sometimes peer pressure can pay off. As the song ends, I get a hug and walk off the dance floor. At least the butterflies are gone now. I blink.

I open my eyes as I walk up the bleachers. The upper classmen chant in unison, "Go home, freshmen!" I wish I were not a freshman. The other students are always so tough on us. The chants turn into cheers.

The crowd roars with cheers for our junior varsity football team. I am a sophomore now, and I have never played a sport as hard as I play football. There is nothing like getting rid of stress by hitting the person in front of you when it is for a friendly game. I get hit so hard that I land flat on my back.

I reach out to get up, but instead I grab the steering wheel of my brother's car. There is nothing more nerve-racking than driving for the first time. I think I showed that snowbank who is boss, though! After a few mistakes, practice makes perfect; I pull into my driveway with a sigh of relief and slide back into the seat.

I sit back up as they call my name. I walk slowly as everyone claps for me. I shake my principal's hand with my right hand as I take my diploma in my left hand. I turn toward my friends and family and hold my diploma over my head. I've finally done it, and it all seemed like a flash. What I wish I had known about becoming a teenager is how fast the years go by so that I could have lived and enjoyed it to the fullest.

Alexander Walker

Being a Teen

## A Beautiful World

High school is a passage of time
In which we find our world unwind.
Our hopes are crushed, our dreams trodden.
We mope around, but we've forgotten
We live in a beautiful world.

Gray matter is squashed, melted, and smushed
Due to tumultuous amounts of work.
Boyfriends. Girlfriends. They come, they go.
They make us happy. Then sad ever so.
We live in a beautiful world.

Home is a bust. We live in mistrust.
We want. We want. We want.
We whine. We shout. We yell. We complain.
"I hate you," we often proclaim.
We live in a beautiful world.

Although it's a drag, we still must go on
Living out life to its fullest.
Although there are bad times,
There are also good times.
Just remember,
We live in a beautiful world.

Melissa Jensen

**Being a kid** is great, but being a teenager is even better.

Christopher Iadicicco

**Being a teenager** is a hard but very cool job. It is hard because you are not an adult yet so you don't get all those privileges, but you are not a baby either. So you are just "stuck" for a couple years. But these "stuck" years have been the best of my life. I have made friends that will last a lifetime. These are the years that I hope I will look back on with no regrets and maybe a couple of laughs. Getting older means more stress and harder decisions. But the best thing about growing up is that you get to make those decisions. In the teenage years you are discovering who you are as a person and trying not to leave the child within you behind. The best thing about the teenage years, besides boys, driving, and going to college, is the mystery of it all. Know that you create your own destiny, and you alone control where the car of life takes you. So drive it well and don't forget to put on your seat belt.

Erin Davis

## Everything Is Temporary

I had a little mantra when I started high school—a phrase that I kept in my back pocket and referred to often: "Everything is temporary." I repeated it quietly on nights when it seemed as though I could work forever and never finish all the things that needed doing. I wrote it in my journal when fights with friends seemed like the end of my social life as I knew it. My little mantra comforted me because I knew it was true—no matter how frus-trated I was, I was sure to be fine in a week—two weeks at the most. It always worked out that way. A senior now, I realize that "Everything is temporary" applies to good things as well as bad. The friendships I have now are not the friendships I had, nor will they remain as they are. There's nothing anyone can do about it—everything, good and bad, ends or changes. Don't worry about the bad—it passes. Remember the good stuff before it's gone and you realize you missed it. Everything is temporary, and that's okay.

Sarah Lang

**On one fateful** summer's day I packed up my Beanie Babies, dolls, and stuffed animals, threw them in the attic, and said a final goodbye to my childhood.

About two weeks later I realized this was not the way to let go. I started asking myself questions about life and growing up. What's so bad about childhood? Why do so many teens spend their time running away from it, pushing it away like some leper? I came to the conclusion that my childhood wasn't something to run away from, it was something to embrace. The thought of maturing, of growing up, had overwhelmed me for the worst. Breaking free of the chains of maturity, I reverted back to my childhood. I began to love the things that made childhood so pure for me: sunflowers, rabbits, playing outside, riding bikes, eating ice cream, and just being happy. And in doing so, I faced and conquered the biggest challenge of becoming a teenager—not letting go of my childhood, but embracing it.

Here's what I suggest you do: take solace in the things that bring you comfort. And by that I mean don't grow up too soon and forget your childhood. That's what's wrong with most teens and adults today. They ran away from their childhood, and when they sought to find it again, it had left them. By keeping your childhood near you, you learn that it's all right to cry or feel happy for no reason, to dance and run until the sun falls in the fiery blaze we often look to on the horizon for reassurance. Don't grow up too fast, and don't leave your childhood behind.

Renate Seiwert

# Being Yourself

**I joined the soccer team,** and we had conditioning and practice almost every day that summer before my freshman year. Before school even started, I had met a lot of girls from all grade levels, but none of them really knew me. I made the varsity team, so I was playing with juniors and seniors, and this intimidated me. I hardly said two words to anybody that summer. I was too scared. I was scared that they wouldn't like me, or that I would say something stupid, or that they would make fun of me. This fear kept me not only from being myself but from being anybody at all. I would simply come to practice, do what was asked of me, and then return home, hardly showing any spark of personality or any indication that I was having fun. I was too scared that my personality wasn't good enough to be friends with these girls.

This was the biggest mistake I could have made. I realize now that to hide who you are out of fear that some people may not like you is a terrible mistake. Let your personality shine through in everything you do. You cannot possibly please everybody, so there will always be some people who just do not appreciate you for who you are, but that is okay because to make up for it, you will have made the most amazing friends in the world. You cannot afford to let that opportunity pass you by.

Kerri Gramling

**The toughest** aspect of high school has been to unearth and maintain a healthy balance between being accepted and being myself. As an introverted individual, it has been difficult to step out of my shell and let my classmates see who I truly am. When you enter high school, use the opportunity to let your personality, in its entirety, shine through, and develop friendships with people who accept you for who you are without asking you to change.

It is easy to succumb to the pressures of popularity and desire for acceptance. While you may be thinking, as most also think, that those pressures to change yourself by altering wardrobe, hairstyle, favorite television show, etc., will float by you, you are sadly mistaken. For me, it was and still is a constant struggle with myself.

Although I cannot tell you a fail-proof solution to this intricate dilemma, I can suggest that it is helpful to have a good foundation of personal values, to know your limitations, and to know who you are as an individual. A major part of your high school experience will be an opportunity to grow, mature, and discover yourself. It will not always be easy, but if you can have the confidence to be uniquely you, it can be a most amazing, satisfying time of your life.

Eileen Hansen

**My hardest challenge** as a teenager is defining myself. I have often wondered exactly what my purpose is.

Nick Szugye

**The most important** part of being a teenager is to find out who you are.

Emily Lien

**If by some** miraculous inspiration I'd write a giant thesaurus for teenagers, I imagine the list of synonyms for *conformity* I would compile would outnumber the list for every other word. There would be the usual synonyms, like *compliance* or *agreement* or *similarity,* but I think I'd have to add to Roget's traditional version. I'd have to add *survival, bewilderment, wishful thinking, idealism,* and, of course, *disillusionment.* Being a teenager is surrounded by a growing myth that complete transformation from a junior high ugly duckling to the teenage beautiful swan is the storybook journey that every teenager must make. And, of course, in order to follow in the perfect path of transformation, you have to look like, dress like, act like, and be like every other self-proclaimed teenage swan. Fortunately, I've learned that this storybook journey is simply fiction, because the idea that complete conformity brings a happy ending is wishful thinking for people who are too scared to finish writing their own story.

But my thesaurus for teenagers wouldn't be complete without associating conformity with a little healthy inspiration. True friends—the kind who never force you to change into something you question or challenge—can be a great, positive source of inspiration. Friends can give you the perfect examples of healthy conformity, whether it's deciding what movie to rent on a Friday night, trying a new hobby, or buying that new CD. But once fitting in no longer means being who you are, conforming means letting yourself be shaped into someone other than your true self and then neither you nor others will be able to tell who you really are.

Maggie Waltz

**Image and appearance** become more and more important as one grows older, at least this was how it was for me. When I was a freshman, I was so concerned with how I looked and acted around my peers. I was more concerned with what my peers thought of me than how I felt about myself. I was always thinking to myself, "Krista, you need to hang out with the right people, you need to buy the right clothes, you need to talk the right way." I was so obsessed with these kinds of thoughts that I spent more time doing absolutely nothing and less time actually living a life.

Now, four years later, I look back and compare my life from then to now and I see a huge change. I have learned a very valuable lesson. It may sound cliché, however it is true, that the only person you need to worry about impressing is yourself.

The advice I am trying to give you is not that you are the only one that matters and no one else in the world is important, or that you should be a loner and not make friends. I have made friends, great friends, friends that will be very dear to me until the day I die. No, that is not what I am saying at all. The advice I am offering to you from my personal experiences is this: love yourself first, then others will love you, for you.

Krista Anderson

**My best advice** is to be yourself. Trying to lie and be someone or something you're not will get you in trouble and believe me, I know. Never be ashamed of who you are or who your friends are (no matter how weird people think they are).

Timothy Balaquiot

**The odds** were against me when I began high school: how could I stand out and get people to notice me? I knew not one person out of the 635 students, almost all of whom were smart and gorgeous. Having uniforms, identification numbers, and the same gender didn't help either. Did I mention I was one of eleven Megans? I began to see my quest for individuality as a waste of time.

Wanting an adventure, I joined my school's rowing team. Suddenly I was surrounded by frightened girls like me wanting so badly to fit in, yet still wishing to hold on to what made them unique. Not only did I make a ton of friends, I fell in love with the sport and was exceptionally good at it. I had discovered my ticket to success and individuality; I even had medals and friends to prove it.

As the days passed, I began to view my peers in a different way. Their special talents and abilities stood out, and girls were called "Emily, who has an amazing voice" instead of "student number 507." We were all succeeding in making our mark at our school, and everyone was doing it in her own unique way.

Megan Costic

**When I was younger,** I had one big worry; it was something called puberty. As a male, my voice started to crack and I also grew facial hair. I had to start shaving and I talked less. After I passed this emotional barrier (which I call embarrassing), being a teenager became fun. My voice stopped cracking and became deeper, and shaving, please, it is easy.

Michael C.

**Crazily enough,** I thought I could be perfect. I thought I could get great grades, be friends with everyone, win the game, star in the play. . . . I figured I could do it all. It wouldn't be like grade school, and I would be different. I wouldn't make mistakes. That was the wrong attitude to start out with. Looking back, I wish I knew to be myself and have fun.

When I turned thirteen, it was a week before eighth grade. I lost my glasses and got contacts. I had my braces put on and my hair highlighted over the summer. I was all ready for school. I imagined I would start out the year with a new slate. I was in eighth grade. I was a teenager. I could be popular and everything would be perfect! Though, of course, all the embarrassing moments from before weren't erased, and walking in on the first day with a huge grin didn't automatically earn me a seat at the best lunch table. I was desperate, I had to be cool, and I had to be perfect. My parents needed good grades; I wanted to go out on the weekends with the popular kids. So I was willing to try anything. Fake trends, act like I knew about a certain music group, or even dress a certain way. I was so busy being something I wasn't, I didn't even know who I was. On top of all that, I was miserable, and day after day it was only getting worse.

Finally I graduated, thought I had matured, and now was really ready to be cool. I dyed my hair, bought new clothes, and made sure I listened to all the big bands. I tried to talk and laugh with just about every girl in my class and considered every one of them a friend. When they asked about a rapper I had no idea about, I would just nod and smile, talking about how much I loved him. Of course, everyone saw through me. No one wanted me in their little clique, and I felt like a total outcast. I couldn't think of what I was doing wrong. I wondered why I didn't have friends and why I was working so hard for these people who didn't seem to care at all. That's when reality hit. Just at the end of my freshman year, it started sinking in. Slowly, I dropped the act. I regretted everything and felt like I had missed out on so much. I can honestly say I hate that I acted so fake.

I thought I could be the perfect student too. I tried so hard to get perfect grades. I stayed up late making sure I studied at least two hours for every test and completed every assignment perfectly. I ignored my own opinions so much that I didn't even develop them for a while, just soaking up everyone else's and recycling them to use again later. Every little thing I failed at set me back. I didn't make the musical, or the volleyball team, or even the cheerleading squad. Those small setbacks really tore at me and wore me down to a point where I just gave up.

I decided it wasn't worth it, trying so hard to be perfect. I wanted to live, enjoy my years . . . and learn who I was. I still don't know who I am, and sure life isn't perfect. It's not supposed to be. I listen to what I want, dress how I want, and I found people who accept me for it. I can accept them for who they are too, even though we rarely agree on anything. I may not be friends with everyone, but I do talk with people outside my lunch table. It seems so silly to say, and think about, since everyone is always reinforcing the statement "Be original." But it is true. You can't be something you aren't. Happy, false images don't attract people; they drive them away. I'm glad I learned this lesson though, because it helped me become who I am today and to appreciate myself for my talents. I am nowhere near perfect. But now I happen to at least know I can try. Then if I fail, I can try again. No one is perfect, and no one can be. If I had known not to try to be perfect and just to be myself before becoming a teenager, things would have been a lot easier.

Sarah Robinson

**Identity.** A few years ago, that word had little, if any, meaning in my life. I just wanted to be a "normal" adolescent kid. I tried to wear the right clothes, say the right things, and was swept up in the endless quest to be a part of the "in" crowd. Now, several years later, as I eagerly await college acceptance letters and count down the days until I move out and enter the real world, I look back on those times and I cringe. What do I wish I had known about becoming a teenager? I wish I'd known that it was okay to be me.

What does the word *normal* even mean? Think about it. Merriam-Webster's dictionary says, "conforming to a type, standard, or regular pattern." This is what I strived to be? Conforming to a standard? Ordinary? Unfortunately, like most people my age, it was. I remember the first day I entered junior high. I had followed all the dress code rules. My shoes were only an inch high, my blouse all the way buttoned, my shirt completely tucked in, and yes, I'll admit it, my skirt at knee level. Naturally, from day one, I was labeled a dork. From that point on, I spent my middle school years striving to overcome this label, trying to be one of the cool kids. Within a week, I'd convinced my mom to buy me new, chunky heels, I made sure to untuck my shirt as soon as I got on the bus, and I'd mastered the art of rolling the waistband of my skirt.

To my dismay, I never became one of them. And now, I am glad. Gradually, I've come to my senses and realized that anyone I have to impress isn't worth impressing. I know now that if someone cannot accept and embrace me for who I really am, then they're not worth it. Today I would never even consider changing just to be like someone else. I am glad that I'm different. I wear whatever I want to, regardless of what the latest fashion is. I'm not afraid of looking silly; I do what's fun. I play board games, I watch Disney movies, and I wave to crossing guards. I'm not afraid of getting dirty, or of messing up my hair. I love football, I ride horses, and I skip around in the rain. I tuck in my shirt, and I'm proud of it. Ordinary? No, not me.

Katie Guardino

## Mirror, Mirror

One of the biggest challenges a teenager faces today is how to feel comfortable with who you really are and the gifts that God has given you. There are many physical changes taking place within your body that you have to learn to cope with. Many of these changes do not coincide with the image of the stereotypical teenager that appears on television or graces the covers of popular teen magazines. Questions such as these—Are my teeth white enough? Is my hair straight enough? Am I thin enough? Are my clothes in style?—are always on your mind. There is enormous pressure to look perfect with a flawless complexion and a gorgeous tan all year long. Validation from friends and peers can become an obsession. The only way to successfully meet this challenge is to focus on your positive qualities. It is also important to find real friends who accept you for who you are. Sometimes you must move from one group to another to find the right fit. This is not easy; it takes a lot of courage and is very stressful. However, it is well worth the grief to find friends who will accept you just the way you are, flaws and all. It is only through these kinds of relationships and positive self-assessment that you will find an inner happiness. This is the feeling that allows you to look in the mirror on a bad hair day with your skin broken out and still be able to smile and have a great day.

Stephanie Wolff

**Don't change** yourself to try to fit in, because it doesn't work.

Brandon Leddy

## What Do You See?

When you look in a mirror, what do you see?
I see more than just my reflection looking back at me.
Look past the eyes, so perfectly lined
And the lashes coated in mascara of the expensive kind.
Look past the hair, either straight as a pin
Or you've spent half the night with your hair curlers in.
Look past the outfit, off the pages of *Seventeen*.
Maybe for just one day skip your daily routine.
Look past your reflection to the person you are.
Do you have the talent to be a movie star?
Perhaps the brain of a doctor you see
Or the shrewd business skills of the apprentice on TV.
Maybe you'll argue my case in court
Or you will play a professional sport.
When you look in the mirror, see more than your hair.
Your own potential is what's standing there.

Brittany Mazzatto

**Learn** to express yourself, learn to learn, and learn to teach. The ones that you affect will see you for who you are and will learn from your way of thinking. You cannot change any of this. You are who you are; you will never be anyone else. Don't abuse it; it is the greatest gift you will ever know.

Lauren Devany

**Being a teenager** is a time to learn about yourself and become closer to the person that God is intending you to be.

Alicia Trautman

**When I entered** high school, I experienced somewhat of an identity crisis. I began to become uncomfortable with my self-image and lacked an understanding of who I truly was. It was at this point that I realized confidence in one's self is the key to being a happy teenager. This idea may seem simple at first, but I have found it extremely difficult to master. Even at sixteen years old, I am still burdened with self-doubt. However, I have made great strides since first becoming a teenager.

Entering high school as a new student was the most frightening experience of my life. My once secure and carefree demeanor became awkward and tense. I was unable to trust my new classmates, and I doubted my intelligence. I was uncomfortable with the way I looked, and I was unsure of my overall self-image. In my heart, I knew this was not the real me. I needed to restore my energetic spirit.

By confronting my fears of life and learning to modestly praise my achievements, I was able to learn how to become a more confident individual. I am now more inclined to speak my mind and believe in myself. There are still times when I am unsure of myself, but I now know that confidence is the key to overcoming an obstacle of self-image. I didn't need to be warned about my teenage years. All I really needed to know about becoming a teenager is that confidence will conquer all.

Lily Mercer

*Being Yourself*

**Steph giggled** hysterically as I frantically stuffed my mother's bra back into the drawer. I glared at her as I scrambled to hide the oranges we had brought upstairs. I could feel my face getting red as I pictured what my mother would say if she knew we had been parading around the house, fantasizing that the citrus fruits under our shirts were actually womanly curves. I slid down onto the floor, tugging violently at the worn gray carpet in my hallway. I was so frustrated with my body. All I wanted was to have something to fill out my bikini top, but like everything else that seemed worthwhile to my eleven-year-old mind, I would just have to wait until I was older.

"This is so unfair," I whined. "My cousin started wearing a bra in fourth grade, and she actually needed it!" I knew that whining and wishful thinking would not cause any desired growth, nor would eating pickles or bananas like some of the girls in my class had said.

I trudged into my bedroom, taking a hopeful glance at my profile as I passed the mirror. As usual, there was no surprise addition to my shape. I was convinced that these daily inventories would speed up my physical development, but sadly, I had no such luck. I flopped on my bed and closed my eyes, comforting myself with unrealistic images of the future. I always found myself imagining a stunning teenage girl a few years older than me. I was convinced that with the passing of time, I would inevitably transform into this magical creature known as the sixteen-year-old girl. My figure, skin, and wardrobe would be flawless, and boys would appear out of nowhere to take me out on Saturday nights. The sound of my mother coming up the steps shook me out of my fantasy, but I kept my eyes closed in order to avoid the awkward explosion of giggles that would occur when Steph and I were asked what we did while she was gone.

I spent a lot of my youth in front of that mirror, wishing some things away, and longing desperately for some features that I did not have. No matter how hard I stared, or how many times I wished, the girl staring back at me was rarely what I wanted to see. As I got older, I matured and developed into a young woman. While I know my eleven-year-old self would have been ecstatic with a few of the physical changes, my sixteen-year-old self came to realize that none of the true signs of beauty and womanhood would ever appear in my reflection. Waiting around to grow up was a difficult task, but coming to the realization that the size of the orange I put in my bra is less important than the amount of patience and compassion I possess made it well worth the wait.

Molly Dougherty

**Being yourself** means that you do not have to follow others. So do not try to be someone that you are not. This also means that you don't try things that you would not normally do because someone you know is doing it. Do things for yourself and be comfortable with your actions. Remember, the original is better than the copy.

Samuel Williams

**I think** the most surprising thing of all coming into my teenage years was the way I slowly got to know myself. I became my own best friend.

Rose Ashe

**Every day seems** to be Halloween for today's teenagers. We wear so many masks, I wonder where the real part of us is.

Kimberly Tippin

# Dealing with Peer Pressure

**People older than you** say peer pressure is not good for you and that it will hurt you. But you may say, "Not me, I won't follow peer pressure, no one can make me do something that I don't want to do." However, things like drugs, media, and most of all friends help sneak peer pressure in.

A big part of peer pressure is wanting to fit in and to be accepted and loved. Believe it or not, peer pressure usually starts between first and fourth grade. With girls, it starts with the Barbie stage. On show 'n tell day when you bring your Barbie dolls to school and all the other girls have stuffed animals and jewelry, they make fun of you and say, "Barbie dolls are for little girls." With boys, it's when you and your mom go shopping for underwear and you see some of your friends and you think nothing of it. But next Monday in school, the kids make fun of you because someone saw your mom picking out your underwear. So then you are pressured to get rid of all your dolls and to stop shopping with your mom even if you don't see the problem with it, all because of the peer pressure and the desire to fit in. This is just the beginning. One day it's Barbie, the next it's pot, and then the day after that it's sex.

I wish I would have known that it's not vitally important to be accepted or liked by everyone. If you change everything about yourself to fit what others want you to be, then you're not you anymore.

Faith Kierra Parker

**Some peer pressure** is subtle, which makes it hard to recognize and fight. One of the best ways I have found to battle teen peer pressure is to find an adult that you trust enough to be open with. It gives you a person to talk to and get valid practical advice from. They have lived longer than you and have surely gone through similar struggles with peer pressure. By telling them your problems, you may get advice that helps give you the inner strength to fight peer pressure.

The best way to beat peer pressure is to value things other than being accepted by your peers. You must first and foremost value yourself. Find out what you believe in and stick up for it if it is compromised. Don't let others run or ruin your life.

Laura Johns

**One of my biggest worries** about teenage life was dealing with peer pressure. I knew there would be kids offering me cigarettes and trying to get me to do other stupid things. I didn't know how I was going to be strong and say no. I honestly thought that I might wither under the pressure. What I found out soon enough is that the solution to this problem is simple. Just say NO! If this isn't as easy for you as it was for me, then just think to yourself, "Do I want to ruin my life?" The answer to this question should be no for everyone.

Chris Sodano

**The best thing** to fight pressure is to know who you are and what you believe in.

Hannah Basting

**Many of my** trying situations took place between sophomore and junior year. I had found my best friends; they felt the same way in return. Or so I thought. One of the biggest falsehoods about high school is that the friends one makes freshman year will be there for all four years. A person is very lucky if they are able to maintain a friend for all four years of school. However, that is normally not the case.

My friends were the wrong friends for me to have. They were leading me down the wrong paths in life. I had entered a world of uncertainty, and all I knew was that I didn't want to be there. I was lost; they were the only friends I had, and I was scared of being alone, so I played along.

Another misconception is that "all the cool kids are doing it." Well, really, they aren't. It's okay to say no to peer pressures. More and more kids are saying no every day, and no one will look down upon them for it, unless they are not a true friend.

Finally, I decided to leave my "best" friends. I was alone. To be alone is probably one of the scariest things, but it is possible. God was there for me to fall back on, and led me to a new friend, one who cares for me and respects me in ways that I had never felt with my "best" friends. I had finally come to find God's grace. After being led down the wrong path by people I deeply admired, being alone, picking myself up from the mess, and finding a new friend, I had finally found myself, and without God, it would not have been possible.

Erin Brossia

**Negative peer pressure** during the teen years can be rather strong. Sometimes people pretend to be your friend and try to get you to do the wrong things. In order to deal with negative peer pressure, you must set boundaries for yourself that you are not willing to pass. When someone tries to push you beyond those boundaries, you have to be ready to tell him or her to stop. You must be courageous and stand up for your beliefs.

Jennifer Colla

**I have found** that since I surround myself with a good group of friends and have passions that are important to me, the peer pressure to use drugs and alcohol is easily overcome.

Beth Brownson

**One day** in the school yard, some kids came up to me and wanted me to try the weed they were smoking. I told them no and walked away. Sometimes other kids may try to bully you into smoking with them. You must always be strong enough to say no. If this ever happens to you, you have to say no and walk away. Smoking weed will never solve any of your problems or make you feel better. If you are feeling very stressed, then you need to talk to someone and ask for help.

Steven Bohanno

**When you realize** your friends are pressuring you to do wrong things, then they probably aren't your true friends.

Abby Lucas

## Don't Give In

Ever since I turned thirteen, I have been learning how to deal with being a teenager. There have been many tough times. I've watched friends travel down the wrong path, and I've seen enough drama to last me a lifetime. I've also dealt with a lot of peer pressure, but each time I face that challenge and don't give in, I become a stronger person and it's easier for me to say no. Peer pressure is definitely one of the biggest challenges that all teenagers face nowadays. More kids need to learn to just not give in. There are ways to deal with it too. Try to find a morally good group of friends to hang out with, listen to what your parents tell you, and stick with your faith.

Faith is yet another struggle for many, many teenagers. This is often the time of religious questioning. Why should I believe if there's no proof? What's the point of going to Mass? No one else does. Luckily, I've been able to go to Mass every weekend, and I've managed to hold on to my faith. From my experience, I highly recommended that you don't follow the crowd and say, "Forget religion." As long as you don't give in to peer pressure and you hang out with the right crowd, high school will be an unforgettable experience and you'll be proud of yourself for doing what's right.

Christine

**To prevent** peer pressure you should choose your friends carefully. Don't choose friends that do drugs and party all the time. It will just lead you into a big mess. Peer pressure affects you in so many ways, and it all depends on the way you handle it. You have to be careful because sometimes it can ruin your plans for the future.

Sarah Bugansky

**Negative peer pressure** is extremely strong during the teenage years of one's life. To deal with it, teenagers should understand that the person who you are individually is much more important than what society and peers want you to be.

Elise Petras

# Making Friends

**Deciding who** your friends are can be difficult. It might be of benefit for you to develop some sort of personal grouping system of your friends, and then the group they fall into will determine how strong an influence you allow them to have in your life. One possible classification scheme might be as follows:

1. *Not your friends.* People you usually don't associate with under normal circumstances.

2. *Acquaintances.* This group of people includes those you might see in school but that you don't associate with out of school. You might occasionally cross their path out of school, but you wouldn't normally seek them out.

3. *Wannabe friends.* These are people you might want to be friends with for some selfish reasons, such as hoping to be more popular. People who fall into this category are not your true friends because the foundation for the friendship does not have a solid basis.

4. *True friends.* These are the ones in the small, close group of people that you confide in, and you know that they have your best interest in mind. The people in this group are those whose influence on your life makes you a better person.

Knowing who to listen to and who to avoid is the biggest step in fighting unwanted, negative peer pressure. Remember, it's your life and you are responsible for determining what you make of it!

Nicole Adragna

**The one** most important discovery that I've made about making and keeping friends is that you should always do what you think is right and what your heart tells you to do, not what people are pressuring you to do. I unfortunately learned that valuable lesson the hard way. When I started high school, I picked my friends quickly and we hung out and did all the stuff that everyone else was doing on the weekends, but eventually I started getting into a little more trouble than I would have liked. My mom kept telling me that I needed to make a careful and conscious decision about who my friends were and what they were asking me to do, but of course because she was my mom I didn't listen to her. Eventually I realized for myself that the people I had picked to be friends with were not the type of people for me to be hanging out with. I realized that I had known this for a long time but didn't want to stop being friends with them for the fear of becoming less popular or having people think I was uncool. Finally I made the conscious decision to find a new group of friends, ones who wouldn't pressure me to do things I wasn't comfortable with. I found new friends who were a little more low-key, and I realized that they were what I had needed from the start. This was the biggest lesson that I learned throughout high school—to be able to stand up for yourself and make a decision without worrying about how it's going to affect your popularity level. Making good friends who will help you grow in a positive way is a very important aspect of high school, and everyone should be careful not to get involved with the wrong crowd.

Jenny Coppedge

**One discovery** I've made about making friends is that some people accept you for your money, clothes, and externals, but true friends will always accept the real you.

Elise Petras

**The best** advice I can give any preteen is to make good friends you can trust and keep them close.

Chris Siebel

**When I was ten** years old, my teenage sister had a party for all her friends. During the party I had the chance to talk to some of my sister's friends and to hang around and watch them up close. They seemed so cool to me because they were wearing nice clothes and had cell phones. Watching how much fun they had joking around with each other made me want to become a teenager and be just as cool as all of them.

Here I am five years later and am now realizing that it is not as simple as it seemed back then. I realize that having a cell phone and the freedom to do all the cool stuff that teenagers can do comes with a lot of responsibility. As you get older you have to do things on your own. Sure, being a teenager is fun and exciting, but you must know how to make good decisions and how to decide what is right and wrong.

One of the most shocking things that hit me when I became a teenager is peer pressure. Many teens get sucked in and make wrong decisions. I believe that the most important decision that teenagers can make is who they pick as friends to hang out with. When I was seven there was no thought involved in this. I was with my cousins and whoever my mother brought me around. Now it is totally up to me who I hang out with. I choose my friends carefully. I see some of my schoolmates hang out with kids that just try to act cool and nasty, and I have no time for any of that. Being a teen is not as easy as it seemed when I was a young kid, but it is still a great time in my life, and I plan on making the most of it and doing the best that I can.

Michael Carney

**When you become** a teenager, some people will tell you that it's really important that you get into a relationship with a guy or a girl and go out and stuff like that. Let me tell you from personal experiences, it isn't important at all. Now there are really good things that come from these relationships and really bad things. A good thing from having a relationship like this is that you can become very close with someone and you can share your feelings with them. A bad thing is that it can go too far and serious results will come up that you won't be ready for. Now what a lot of young teenagers think is that when they get into a relationship with someone, they will end up marrying that person. In some cases it happens, but most of the time it doesn't. If the person breaks up with you, don't feel like your life is over and that you have nothing to live for.

Seth Capela

**The finest advice** I could give to any individual is to find friends whom you can entrust your life to and keep them close to you.

Mike Czajka

**Do you worry** too much about making or keeping your friends? Do you let your friends make decisions for you? Have you ever done something you knew was wrong just because your friends were doing it?

Friends are an important part of life, but you should not base what you do on what they do. When I was younger, I always wondered what others thought of me, and I based many of my decisions on what my friends said and did. I would do things I really did not feel like doing or hang out with people I really did not like, just because that was what everyone else was doing. It was almost as if I were wearing a costume. I acted like a completely different person when I was around my so-called friends. I was not happy with myself. I was tired of acting like everyone wanted me to and doing what they wanted me to do. You can only be someone you are not for a short time before your true self comes out. When I stopped doing what my friends wanted and stopped acting like my friends did, I was no longer part of the popular group. I threw the "costume" away. Many of my friends, or those I thought were my friends, stopped talking to me and stopped including me in things. But that was okay with me because I made new friends, the kind that like you for who you are. I didn't have to do things I did not want to do, or hang out with people I really did not like; all I had to do was be myself. These are your true friends. If you have to hide any part of yourself to fit in, then you really need to take a look at your friends and even more, yourself. No one is happy being someone else, so don't try and make yourself someone you are not. Don't put on a costume. You will thank yourself later.

Dominique Santiago

**Boys** are not your whole world. Even though you may want them to be, they never will be. I'm not saying it's not okay to have a boyfriend. It is absolutely okay. Just don't make him your whole world.

Semaj Saucier

**Today's teenage** social system is based entirely on popularity. In other words, the more friends you have the better. My parents always told me that all I really need is one good friend. I didn't listen to them, and I fell right into a trap. I believed that the more friends I had, the more popular I would become. I never thought for a moment that the kids I was hanging around with might not even like me in return. All I cared about was that I had friends and that people noticed. As I progressed through ninth grade, I noticed that it was getting harder to do schoolwork. My grades started dropping, and I was facing troubles not only in school but out of school as well. I started looking to my supposed "friends" for help. They just ignored me and went on with their daily lives. That is all except for one, a young boy by the name of Tom (I've changed his name for the sake of privacy).

As my grades started dropping in school, so did my morale. I started thinking that everything was hopeless and that no matter what I did it wouldn't help. Tom stood by me and encouraged me to keep it up and told me that if I tried hard enough I could dig my way out of this pit I had dug for myself. I tried to look enthusiastic about it, but I never really caught on to what Tom was telling me until later. One night when I was home alone, I contemplated whether I should just end it all, just give up and take the easy road out. For me it looked as though that was the only solution to the problem I faced. Then as I sat there pondering my situation, the phone rang. I picked it up and on the other end was Tom. He spoke to me about some trouble that he had been having and how he thought he was a complete failure at life. Then he told me that he stuck with it and eventually was able to come back on top. We talked on the phone for about an hour and a half. That hour and a half I will never forget, for it was in that hour and a half that Tom saved my life. He turned my whole perspective of life around. He told me that he would help me through the tough parts, and all I had to do was work for it.

As time went on, our friendship strengthened. No matter what kind of trouble I got myself into, Tom was always there to help me out. He was the light that helped guide me through my endless hours of darkness. I am forever in debt to Tom for what he helped me through, and no matter how I act or what I do, he always sees me for who I really am. I guess it's true what they say: true friends are hard to find, difficult to leave, and impossible to forget.

Anthony Forneris

**My advice** to someone entering this phase of life would be never to judge anyone by the way they look.

Kristen Obey

**Friends help** you through tough times, respect you, support your decisions, and tell you when you are doing wrong things, because they don't want to see you get hurt. Just remember, don't let anyone change you into someone you're not. Don't let anyone degrade you, and most of all, just be yourself.

Abby Lucas

Making Friends

**When I was younger,** my life was my family and my schoolwork. I will always love my father and mother, always quarrel with my brother and sister, and always enjoy learning and working hard in school. I was, and still am mostly, a shy, quiet person. I rarely talked or played with anyone in school on a regular basis. I kept to myself except for occasional conversations with classmates. My definition of a best friend had been the person I talked with the most in school. I had one friend where we would go places and to each other's houses. I was fine with my life that way. A social life was not an issue to me.

Then when I was twelve or thirteen, people changed, and I found out what the world is really like. I found that "always" doesn't always last for everything.

Honestly, I don't know much about teenage life. When my classmates in seventh and eighth grade started to go from childhood to adolescence, I didn't. I never knew what being a teenager was all about. I stayed to my simple life of school, studying, and anything else that had to do with academics in school. Then the world said, "Hello." People made fun of me, joked about me, and didn't care about me. I was surprised what people said about me, either to others or directly to my face. It still goes on today. Sure, I try to block it out, but day after day, they keep talking, not caring about my feelings. I'm surprised that the people you play freeze tag with in the school yard during the first grade will come up to you a few years later, unfreeze you, and show you what your life is going to be like.

One of the friends I have made in high school told me that this happens to everyone. I hope I make more friends like him in high school.

We should remember that bullying comes in many forms; we should be careful what we say to others.

Owen Colton

# Living Your Faith

**My strategy** for staying close to God is praying and loving all of his people to the best of my ability. I don't always do this well, but I think the fact that I am trying makes God happy and brings us closer. As a preteen, I really didn't grasp all that praying is, but now I really do. Praying is any time you ask for help from God or talk to him. Asking the saints to put in a good word for you with him is also considered praying. There are always the good standbys of traditional prayers that have comforted and helped me through. Having friends who also believe in God whom you can talk to about him helps, though it is not a necessity. Whatever you do, remain as close to God as you can, and never stop believing in him, even if you are angry with him. He will always love you, I promise. He will never leave you alone.

Lizzy Pugh

**Disease,** war, and crime make it difficult to believe in a loving God. It's hard enough to see God in the world, but evil makes the struggle even harder. Belonging to a community of faith has helped me to believe in God though. Spending time with other people that have the same beliefs gives me greater understanding and confidence about my religion.

Michael J. Sanders

**Upon becoming** a teenager, a light switch of sorts turns on. Many—not all, but many—teenagers become very cynical and doubtful of what goes on around them and in the world in general, especially when it comes to religion. Many people say that children never stop asking questions, but I think that saying is better when used to describe teens. Doubting one's faith is a part of life because there are too many unknowns. I've heard the saying that faith is the "evidence of things not seen" (Hebrews 11:1), and that's absolutely true because we can't see what we have religious faith in. We just have to trust that it's there.

John Koneval

**Adolescence** is about growing up and learning. Have fun, but don't forget the true goal, and that is being successful in the long run. I know as well as anyone that all temptations cannot be resisted, but try hard. Never do something because others think it is cool or if you are unsure of the consequences. Always remember God is on your side even when you think you are standing alone. I often say the serenity prayer when I feel lost and need guidance:

God,
grant me the serenity to accept the things I cannot change,
the courage to change the things I can,
and the wisdom to know the difference.

(Reinhold Niebuhr)

Sammie

**Since you will** become busier in your teenage years, make sure that you leave time for God. Try and take some time out of your day, even if it is only fifteen minutes, to just relax and talk with God. This will make your day seem much more calm and stress free. Personally, I pray every night before I go to bed. Choose a time, whether it is in the morning or at night, to share your thoughts and feelings with God.

Erin Roesner

**How can teenagers maintain** an active social life without turning their backs on God or family?

Teenagers can become active in different groups of friends that will support them with their beliefs. Teens can become part of a church youth group or school club that promotes faith and good attitudes. Teenagers can be role models in their community, working with children who are poor or who might need help. Teens can also be active in sports. There are not many clubs that help teens today with good attitudes and spreading God's word, but there are a few you can join, like the Fellowship of Christian Athletes, Students Against Destructive Decisions, Red Cross clubs, and church youth groups or councils.

Jordan McIntire

**Dear God,**

I still feel completely alone. Neither of them has called me, and they used to be my best friends. Why would you let this happen to me? I wasn't the one to stab my best friend in the back. I'm the innocent one, and I am home alone while they're having the time of their lives. Why would you punish me for this when I didn't do anything?

This is the prayer I would cry into my pillow every night over the summer when I felt like God had forgotten me, left me, or worse, punished me. I would spend my days at home waiting for a miracle. If God really loved me, he would take away my pain and bring me a new life.

Miracles don't happen if you're sitting at home watching TV all day. I finally realized nothing was going to happen if I expected God to do everything and did not work with him. I had a new plan of action: I would call up my old friends and rekindle my relationships with them.

After a couple months, I had more friendships than I ever could've imagined. I couldn't be happier about the miracle I helped create with God. What I received wasn't close to what I asked for, it was ten times better!

Meghan McCarthy

## God, Please Prepare Us

God, please
prepare
us, the
children Of God,
on our path
into aDolescence,
and allow
us to make,
decisIons that
will guide ourselves in the right path: O Lord, for you are my faith, my
passion, and my destiny. I promiSe to stay faithful in my heart and
mind,
for I knoW
thAt you, the
Lord, will be wiTh
me on my journey.
of adolesCence.
Help me
to live my
lIfe day by
day aNd
accept the
thinGs that
happen before
me. Amen.

Jim D'Angelo

## Living Your Faith Every Day

One of the biggest responsibilities as you become a teenager is to be true to yourself and stay firm in your morals. You will meet many new people, which is wonderful and very exciting. But some may challenge your morals and question your beliefs. I wish someone would have warned me how hard this would be. A way to make it easier is to surround yourself with a positive group of friends and to understand your life is between you and God—no one else. As you become a teenager, growing closer to God does not mean just praying and going to Church, but truly living your faith in everyday life. When I find this too difficult, I read these words from Mother Teresa. I hope they inspire you.

People are often unreasonable,
illogical, and self-centered;
**Forgive them anyway.**
If you are kind,
people may accuse you of selfish, ulterior motives;
**Be kind anyway.**
If you are successful,
you will win some false friends
and some true enemies;
**Succeed anyway.**
If you are honest and frank,
people may cheat you;
**Be honest and frank anyway.**
What you spend years building,
someone could destroy overnight;
**Build anyway.**
If you find serenity and happiness, they may be jealous;
**Be happy anyway.**
The good you do today,
people will often forget tomorrow;
**Do good anyway.**
Give the world the best you have
and it may never be enough;
**Give the world the best you have anyway.**
You see, in the final analysis,
it's all between you and God;
It was *never* between you and them anyway.

Paige McPhail

## Finding Peace

I have experienced struggles with my faith more often now that I'm a teenager. When something terribly wrong happens in my life, I immediately blame it on God, and I know I shouldn't, but at the time, I'm not thinking reasonably or clearly. I'm simply thinking upon instinct. There have been times when I haven't gone to church for months on end, like when my grandmother died five years ago. I blamed her death on God, I asked why he would take such a beautiful woman from us, right when we needed her most, and how she could leave us all like that, just up and go so suddenly. I didn't go to church for almost six months, but the day that I went back, I was greeted with open arms back into the church, and slowly my grief started to lift, and I realized that with every situation, there can always be something good that comes out of it. Most people don't realize it at the moment something bad happens, but it slowly becomes apparent as time goes by. Now I'm closer to my grandfather, and my drive to succeed is stronger than ever because I know it's what my grandmother wanted. Through every tribulation that I have faced, if I wander away, God always guides me back, and it's there that I find peace with myself and peace with the situation.

Katharine T. Meier

**What I wish** I had known about being a teenager is that it is important to know your faith. Religious and moral issues are a hot topic for discussion among teens, whether in school, youth groups, or in conversation with friends. Don't just believe something and live a certain way because that's what you've been taught. Other teenagers will call you on it. Be prepared to be questioned about your faith. This means making your faith your own. Really get to know the "whys" for what you believe. If you know where you stand, other teens will too and they will respect that. Don't be the person with no answers.

Faith is also important because it gives you something solid to hold on to in a time that can be very confusing. When everything around you seems to be changing so quickly, faith grounds you. The teenage years are full of fun, but they are also full of hard decisions, peer pressure, and numerous temptations. Without something to help you resist these occasions for sin, you will fall more easily. A strong faith will guide you to make good decisions now and for the rest of your life.

Alex Lewis

## Dear God,

You have called your servants to adventures
Of which we cannot see the ending,
By paths as yet unexplored,
Through dangers unknown.

Give us the faith to go out with courage,
Not knowing where we go,
But only that your love is leading us
And your hand supporting us;
Through Jesus Christ our Lord.

Amen.

Billy Svoboda

## God Is Always There

When I turned thirteen, many things in my life started to change. Becoming a teen is harder than being a child in some ways, but easier in others. It means more privileges, but also more responsibilities. There are pressures to do things that you wouldn't normally do, but saying no is easy, as long as you keep God in your mind. It is very important to know God is always there for you. There are times when I am confused and don't know what to do, but I ask for God's help and the situation always gets better. As you get older, relying on God is always the way to go. Doing the right thing might not seem cool at the moment, but as long as you stick with God, nothing can go wrong and everything will be alright in the long run.

Elena

**Life is a precious** gift that comes and goes within a blink of an eye. I have learned that life is fragile that and you have to be careful with the choices you make. I have also learned that God has a plan for each and every one of us, so even if our plans don't work out, his plan will. I have seen people who have had a bad start with their life, but now with the support of their family and the people who love them, they're doing a lot better and getting their lives on the right track. So if you find yourself angry or disappointed in something that didn't work out, just remember that God has something better planned. One other thing I have learned is to dream big, because no matter your age, your size, or your color, you can do whatever you set your mind to, because anything is possible.

Kasy Bennett

## God, Please Watch Over Me

God, please watch over me and help me as I enter into a time in
    my life when I might find myself lost.

Grant me the ability to know where I fit in and to be happy
    with it.
Grant me the strength to know who I want to be and the ability to
    make the decisions that will lead me to be that person.
Grant me the courage to make those decisions as I stand up to
    people who might not agree with them.

Help me fight the pressure from my friends to be someone I
    am not.
Help me fight the pressure from my family, the media, and
    teachers.

Watch over me as I grow into a disciple of your words.
Keep me safe as I try to become someone you want me to be.
Let me hear your words as I go through the day.

Please give me the strength to know that no matter what I do,
    where I go, and what challenges I face, you will always be
    by my side guiding me and holding me as I grow.

*Carolyn Grillo*

## Dear God,

Help me to understand what it is you want me to do as a teen-ager.

Help me to keep my relationships with my friends and family alive and grow even further.

Teach me your ways so I will know what I will need during my teenage years.

Strengthen me so I will not give in to peer pressure and drugs, so my body will be healthy and prepared to work for you, Lord. Keep me prepared to work hard, both physically and academically.

Help me to continue to strengthen my relationship with you, because I will surely need you, and grant me the ability to accept you as my God, even when others may look down on me because of my love for you. Please show me that you love me, even when I am skeptical.

Help me to not become jealous or overconfident in my teenage years, because these attitudes will break down my relationship with you. Also, teach me to understand that grades and popularity are not the most important things in my life, you are.

Most importantly, help me to be as successful as possible. Protect me on my journey through my teenage years and help me to be safe, happy, and spiritual. Thank you, God, for all you have done and all you will continue to do to guide me on my journey as a teenager and in the rest of my life.

Caitlin Stamm

## I Opened My Eyes

I opened my eyes and looked before me and saw my teenage years ahead.

I did not want to embark on this journey, a child I wished to remain instead.

How I was going to get through this I didn't know, for I did not have a plan.

Then I heard God's voice say to me, "I will not forget thee or leave thee, if only you take my hand."

Teenage life was not easy, but there is one thing I can testify, one thing I know for sure.

In spite of the difficulty of these challenging years, God never put more on me than I could endure.

I had some friends and numerous enemies; the boys existed simply to make me cry.

But when times seemed too difficult, I got on my knees and said a prayer, and God wiped every tear from my eye.

I warn you, you'll be teased for silly things like bad hair, clothes, complexion, or imperfect teeth.

But always believe that if you were created by the same God who created the heavens and the earth, then you must be a masterpiece.

Remember that each hair on your head is numbered, and each bone is in its place.

Just continue to abide in the presence of God. Be holy, and stand in his grace.

One of the things I've learned is not to try to grow up too fast because for everything there is a season.

And also, try not to ever question your self-worth or existence. God put us all here for a reason.

Live each day to its fullest, always smile, and never compromise who you are.

But never forget to say a prayer of thanks to the one who brought you this far.

Judith Carline Dolce

## Keep Faith Alive

Keep the faith alive, hold your head up high, there is nothing
you can't get through, with faith in God you will make it
through.
Relationships controlling my every thought, aspect, and move.
Love making me blind and acting out of line.
Heartbreak making me fall apart, hopeless, and bent out of
shape.
However, mutual love makes you feel so blissful and exuberant.
It's the greatest feeling, like being on top of the world.
School stressing me to the point of exhaustion.
The strive for academic excellence has caused distortion.
Brain out of sync since it is being stretched so far.
Although remember it is for a good cause.
Through education comes unimaginable opportunity.
My African American race making me feel at
times inferior or out of place.
Security guards following me in the store to
see that I don't confiscate anything.
Stereotyped as being dumb and less than
everything.
Faith in God is what keeps me uplifted and deeply rooted.
With the Lord by my side, everything is possible,
you want to know why?
God's unconditional love will never lie.
Family matters making me cry.

Mom's death causing me to feel alone and
left scarred.
Crisis building up so much,
resulting in attempting to cross the suicide bar.
"Don't do it! Don't do it!" the angels say.
I stop to think and realize that this is the wrong way out.
Prayer will get you through anything without a
doubt.
Now imagine being teased constantly.
It's making you infuriated or mad.
Also melancholy or sad.
Vendetta or grudge resulting.
Revenge about to occur.
Emotions will be stirred.
Fighting that can become a bullet through the chest.
Tragedy of what could've been prevented
death.
Think before you act.
Solemnly vow to you that with this your life will
stay intact.
Know what you're going through.
Look to God. Search the Bible for answers
and the truth.
Keep the faith alive, hold your head up high, there is nothing
you can't get through, with faith in God you will make it
through.

Britthey Mosley

**On a dark,** beautiful night with visible illuminating stars,
the cool breeze felt comforting as I sat on our porch.
I began reflecting upon my life, which brought back memories of my mother.
I remembered a particular time when she called all of us
to gather around her so she could talk to us.
She told us:

As we live our lives, we must learn to appreciate the little things.
Yes, there are obstacles we will face which might hinder us, but
we must endure.
We must take time to listen to others and observe.
Anyone we come across in our lives can teach us a lesson;
For some have eyes and yet cannot see.
We must perform all tasks with passion and we must have focus;
Everything takes sacrifice and risks, we mustn't let fear overcome
us;
Remember the child of whom you are;
The Bible is your guide.
Remember, you are never alone because God is always with you.

All these words were insignificant at first, but eventually I realized the true meaning.
That night, I prayed for guidance.
Within me I heard a voice:

Enjoy every moment of your life.
God will never give a task to his child if it can't be accomplished.
Remember you are a person of value.
God has planted a seed in you, so recognize it, work on it, and
use it.
Always follow your heart, never accept another's ridicules about
your ways and
keep your head up high.
Never be boastful or take advantage of others.
There are times when we should be quiet.
Have a positive attitude and focus.
Remember to have faith in God.

*Adebola O. Adegbite*

## Dear Lord,

Make me a good teenager. Help me to understand and prevent myself from doing the wrong things that have been done in many other teenage lives. Help me to understand and listen to my parents. Help me to be cautious of the decisions I will make. Help me to learn from my strengths and weaknesses and to develop responsibility. Allow my courage to be strong and keep me from giving in to temptations.

Help me to appreciate the beauty that you have given me and who I am. Help me to not criticize others for their complexion, color, eyes, or hair. I know that in these years of being a teenager, a lot of peer pressure will surround me and I will make mistakes. But help me to learn from those mistakes and become more mature. Lord, you understand the pressure that is upon me. I have so many opportunities in my days, but there is also danger that I must face. Sometimes it is hard to cope with pressures of growing up through our teenage years in today's society. I ask you to give me guidance during difficult times. When I am disheartened or discouraged, look upon me with compassion. Allow me to seek and accept the help of others when needed.

Lord, help me to develop my special talents and to work to my full potential. Help me to achieve the discipline needed to obtain my goals and the courage to pursue my dreams against difficult obstacles. I pray that we all grow intellectually and we listen to your words and follow your example during our teenage years and throughout our lives. We are all your children, and you love us in any shape, form, color, and size. You shelter us in your care, surrounding us with your goodness and enfolding us in your love. Guide us to the peace and serenity found in union with you. Amen.

Melinda Graham

**Dear Lord,**

Help me to keep my memories close
Help me to remember my loved ones the most
Teach me to be confident in all that I do
Show me who I am and how to stay true to you
Remind me that growing up means not too fast
Allow me to make mistakes and learn from the past
Give me guidance, trust, love, and fear
Let me go on my own and always have you near.

Nora Downes Ingersoll

**Faith is an issue** that I have really struggled with as I've gotten older. There are times when I really am not up for going to church on the weekend, but I know I should. As I am getting older, in some ways I feel I am growing apart from God. I tend to spend less time paying attention in Mass and go off into my own world. But you should always stay close to God, because he can help you through the hardest times in your life. One way I have learned to deal with this is by taking a few minutes out of every day to just simply thank God for all he has given me.

Amanda Krolikowski

# Succeeding at School

**Now that I am a teenager,** I feel the pressure bearing down on me like a giant weight on my shoulders, making it hard to see what is really important in life. This pressure makes me want to strive for perfect grades and to be the perfect teen for my parents, but that is an impossible goal. Life is not worth much if you are not loving your neighbors and loving God's creation. God didn't put us here to work, work, work and then die. He put us here to take care of each other. Yes, that involves work, but it involves seeing him in his people too, something that blindly working will not allow you to do.

Lizzy Pugh

**The moment** I entered high school, everything I did became about college. After every sport I played, volunteer effort I made, and grade I received, someone would be right by my side saying either, "Oh! That will look great on a college application!" or, "Uh, you might want to work on that because colleges are going to see it." The pressure to succeed in terms of athletics, academics, and leadership in extracurricular activities is intensified greatly once you walk in the front doors of your new high school. Perhaps the most pressure occurs academically.

Your teachers and guidance counselors will without a doubt remind you repeatedly how much of a role your course grades and SAT scores play in deciding your future. However, many people, especially those same teachers and guidance counselors, fail to address the value of personal and social success. They often do not realize the importance of succeeding in being kind to your friends, respectful of your authorities, and a leader in morality and integrity rather than in the debate club. When you enter high school, it will seem as if your grades do determine the rest of your life, but the honest truth is that they really do not. It is important to show a good work ethic and to attempt to get good grades, but the knowledge that you receive in the long run is really the most important thing.

For me, it is a concept that has taken a long time to grasp, but now I feel more successful when I get a lower grade and do not get upset, than when I get a good grade because I memorized the information twenty minutes before the test. I know now that in the long run, important people in my life, like employers, for example, will not notice the grades I received in high school as much as they notice the knowledge I have acquired or the person that I have become from my experiences.

*Cori Hanky*

**My biggest worry** about becoming a teenager was going to high school. I was scared to go to a new school and meet new kids. I found out that it was not as bad as I thought it would be. There were other kids like me that were scared to go to a new school and meet new friends, so we all fit in nicely. I wish I had known that high school was not as bad as people say it is. My experience so far in my school has been fun, and I have enjoyed it.

Chris Siebel

## Dear God,

The world is a crazy, fast-paced place for a teenager like me. I am just seventeen and already people are expecting me to know what I'm going to do for the rest of my life. I have barely decided what I'm going to do next week, let alone the rest of my life. Even though I am expected to be responsible like an adult, I am still apprehensive and intimidated by our very critical society. There is a lot of pressure to not mess things up, but for me, sometimes that pressure makes me mess up even more. I want to succeed in making a life and career for myself, and I feel that if I don't get all A's on my tests and quizzes and a high score on the ACT, my dreams of someday becoming a doctor will be ruined. Lord, please help teenagers, like myself, not become stressed out by the pressures to succeed. Help us realize that everything happens for a reason, and that if we are truly passionate about something, we will be able to accomplish our goals and aspirations.

Alison Opitz

## I Was Scared

What I had heard about high school is how hard the work was. Everyone told me that I would not have free time. I was scared. I was not the best student in school, and I did not like homework very much. But I soon found out high school was not as bad as I had heard it was. I made many friends within the first few days, and as the year went on, I found the homework was not that bad. There was a lot of homework, but the teachers were there to help us, not hurt us. None of them wants us to fail, but rather they want us to excel.

The teachers who I heard were tough people trying to get us all to flunk out of school were really very nice. They were there to help us with any problems we had and gave us advice. They were my teachers and in a way my friends. High school became so much fun. I loved going to school and even doing homework. My grades also improved. I started passing and excelling in subjects that I was having trouble with. I could not have done this without the help of my teachers. And sometimes I don't know how they deal with us, but they do and they help.

Steven F. Ruggirello

## Keep Trying

When it comes to school you must try, try more, and just keep trying. School is one of the most important things in life. Some people are blessed with the gift of being a great athlete and go to college on athletic scholarships. But if you aren't so great, then you have to rely on your brain to get you to where you want to be in life. I have been told that when you get into high school, you must be sure that you do well your freshman and sophomore years. If you do not, and your junior year rolls around, it is very tough to raise your cumulative GPA, and colleges will not be too pleased with it. So I took their advice into consideration, and I am telling you the same thing. No matter what happens in sports, you should always be on track with your education so you can count on getting where you want to be in life.

Vinnie Fiorilli

## Pressure to Succeed

As much as it pains me to say it, I think I do feel more pressure to succeed as a teenager. It might be that there isn't more pressure being applied, but you start to pick up on it more.

Once in high school, I think you become cognizant of all the pressure that you didn't necessarily pick up on in middle school. Your parents have always wanted you to do well, but now in high school, it seems more important because it will help determine what college you go to. Everything seems more important in high school because it acts as a major determining factor in where you are going to go to college, which essentially sets you up for your life.

I think you as a student also become another source of the pressure that you realize when you hit high school. You start to feel the stress and pressure to succeed. While fueled by teachers and parents, it ultimately comes down to you, the student. You have to decide what's important.

So while becoming a teenager is tough, the pressure you feel increases mainly because you notice it more. You have to decide what is worth it and what isn't worth it. Don't put added pressure on if it's not necessary, and don't stress out on the little, trivial pieces. Decide what's worth your attention and your time, and do those things well.

Elizabeth Green

## Top Ten Necessities for Surviving High School

### 10. Learn to sleep anywhere.

A skill that will come in handy through those classes that never seem to end, and believe me there will always be never-ending classes.

### 9. Get to know the lunch ladies.

When you forget your lunch, they will always be able to find extra food, even if it is only a peanut butter and jelly sandwich.

### 8. Stay close with your friends.

I guarantee that they will be the only ones who will care that you beat the computer at solitaire or not.

### 7. Learn to believe that everything happens for a reason.

Although the current crisis might seem as if it will completely ruin your whole high school career, know that God sends you only situations you can handle.

### 6. Multitask.

Sometimes teachers purposely load on the homework when they know that the season finale of your favorite show is on. The perfect solution is to do your homework during commercials.

### 5. Have fun.

On weekends, when there is no athletic game to go to or no good movie out, just playing Twister or rummy with your friends will be the most fun you will have your high school career.

### 4. Keep a stiff upper lip.

The best defense against gossip is to not let people see how their cruelty affects you. If you accomplish this, their purpose for gossiping about you will be ruined.

### 3. Always keep your sense of humor.

If you do something completely stupid, like trip going up the steps, just laugh and it will take some of the embarrassment away.

### 2. Learn to love the hard teachers.

Every school has the infamous Mr. Smith, in whose class it is harder to get an A than it is to talk to the president. That teacher only wants you to succeed, and when that class is over, I guarantee that you will never regret taking his class.

### 1. Be yourself.

No one likes a phony, so be yourself. Your real friends will like you for who you are, not who you aren't!

*Kathleen Large*

## My Attitude

When I was in middle school, I can clearly remember having no drive and determination for my schoolwork. I guess that type of feeling could be typical for a younger child, who has no concept of what schooling will do for you in the long run, but I know that my parents had to push me a great deal to succeed. Not one grade was won without a struggle, and most of my childhood afternoons were a battle between my parents and me over the completion of my work.

I cannot remember when this occurred, but such struggles stopped taking place. I believe when I arrived at high school, I had what I like to call a revelation. Grades and schooling soon became important to me; I realized how vital grades and my education were to my future. Before my sophomore year, I did not fully comprehend that concept of college either, for such ideas were farthest from my mind at the time. I developed a deep-seated drive though, one that has pushed me until today to work hard and be the best I can be in my academic work and extracurricular activities.

I know I began to succeed when I reached high school, but I do not believe becoming a teenager has put more pressure on me to thrive in school. I suppose that I gained such willingness for success from the maturity I received within my teenage years. The teen years add a lot of stress and importance to your life because you begin to think about your future, so it is understandable that pressure is certainly a feeling that can be obtained. I, on the other hand, want to succeed and strive to be the best I can be—without pressure from my parents and teachers. In these years, I am just thankful that I had the ability to turn my attitude toward education around and make something of my schooling.

Katherine White

# Avoiding Harm

## God's Voice

People are almost always trying to pull you away from who God says you should be, and you have to learn to stand your ground and stay true to who you are and who you were put on earth to be.

As you grow into your teenage years, you may be faced with friends who decide that it's a good idea to experiment with harmful things. They may drink, do drugs, cut themselves, or succumb to an eating disorder. You may think at the time that it may be a good idea for you to get involved too, but it really isn't. You need to be the strong person who stays true to who God made you to be, and help those people in their time of need. In this situation, your friends need you to be the better person and get them some help. Try sitting them down and talking to them about what they are doing and how it is not good for them. Explain to them that what they are doing now affects who they become later on in life. If your message does not seem to get across this way, you may need to involve a responsible adult. Tell your friends that God designed them to be his voice.

Emily Laurel

## Challenges and Choices

Some of the challenges that teenagers face are dealing with drugs, alcohol, and premarital sex. These can be very hard choices to make, because you may think to yourself, "If I don't drink or do drugs or participate in premarital sex, then they won't think I'm cool, and I really don't want to be a loser," or "I won't make the popular crowd if I don't follow through with this." Trust me, this is not true. You will be cool just because you had the guts to stick up for yourself and your beliefs. You are God's creation, and he gave you your own mind to help guide you during tough times like this, and more than likely everyone else is trying to make the same decision. You don't need drugs and alcohol to determine who your friends are, because if the people you call your friends are forcing you into an uncomfortable position, then they are not true friends. Some advice I can give you is to follow your heart and stay away from drugs, alcohol, and sex and find a good group of friends around whom you enjoy being yourself.

Amanda Owens


**If someone's teasing** you about being a goody two-shoes, that's okay. It means you're a good person and you'll go far in life.

Semaj Saucier

**Sometimes you** make new friends who you think are cool and good to hang out with. Eventually you find out that they do drugs or alcohol. These friends, whether cool or not, are not who you want to hang out with. They will drag you down in every aspect of your life. It doesn't matter if they make fun of you. It is better to be right than to do drugs. It will all pass in time.

Brandon Leddy

**I was pressured** by my friends to go smoking and drinking when I was about twelve and thirteen. Instead of doing this with them, I found myself an "antidrug." My antidrug is sports, specifically basketball. I chose basketball because it involves a lot of cardiovascular activity, and if I went out smoking and drinking, there is no chance that I would be able to play basketball for two to three hours a day. So my advice to you is that you should find an antidrug.

Dylan McCann

**Many times** teenagers will fall to the pressure of smoking and drugs. This is usually to fit in with the crowd and feel cool. They are not thinking of the long-term effects these bad habits will have on their bodies. My advice is to learn to say no! No one can argue with a firm NO, and you will probably earn people's respect.

John Picciallo

**If a friend** of mine engaged in risky or harmful behavior, the first thing I would do is try to talk to him or her. I would remind my friend of the dangerous results depending on the situation that he or she is in. If the situation is a drug problem, I would tell the person the consequences, like going to jail or early death. I would also encourage counseling and rehab if it is a very serious problem. If the problem is stealing with a group of friends, I would suggest that the person stop hanging out with them and find other friends that wouldn't steal. Sex is another form of risky and harmful behavior for some teenagers. My solution to that problem would be the same as the other situations and that is to remind that person of the possible results of sexual activity. I would explain the chances of getting diseases such as HIV or AIDS, or even getting pregnant if it is a female friend.

Another piece of advice I would give to a friend of mine who is dealing with risky or harmful behavior is to ask God for help through prayer. I believe that we should turn to God if we ever have problems in our life. Maybe joining a Christian community or a parish would give that person something else to do instead of engaging in whatever the person is going through. If the person is a close friend of mine, I would ask him or her to join me in a worship service on Sundays or even during fellowships on a certain day of the week. Maybe turning to God could change the person's desire to use drugs or steal or engage in sexual acts. I could also suggest looking up certain verses from the Bible that give strength mentally and spiritually. Another option I would consider telling my friend would be to go see a doctor. It is sometimes better to get information from a professional. To help my friend, I could also get that person's family to try and help stop whatever the person's problem is. Maybe words of advice from the people he or she loves could turn the behavior around.

Brian Lam

**Teens are faced** with many opportunities to do drugs, have sex, drink, smoke, and drive recklessly. You may choose to do these things just to be in the "cool" group of people at school, but it isn't cool. It doesn't make you cool to ruin your dreams for the future.

*Brittany*

## Drink or Drive

We got to the house, the music was blaring
but no one seemed to be caring.
What was going on I knew was wrong,
but I did not hesitate to follow along.
I'll just have one is what I thought,
if that's all I have, I won't get caught.
One turned into three or four,
and I did not care anymore.
As I took my seat in the ride,
I think I heard my mother cry.
What I was doing I knew was wrong,
but I just searched the radio for a good song.
I did not consider the driver's condition.
My parents' advice, I should have listened.
As the car sped along,
I knew something was wrong.
The car slid and hit the tree,
and I thought to myself, "This can't be happening to me."
I left the accident with a few bumps and a bruise,
but I learned drunk driving makes my life too easy to lose.
Drunk driving is not a joke,
and the truth is it's okay to have a Coke.

*Brennan Pehotsky*

## Consequences

There are many changes you go through when you become a teenager. You get a later curfew, you start high school, your parents trust you more, and you start dating. There are some changes you must control on your own in order to conquer your teenage years. As you get older, the world becomes more critical. There is a set image of what a teenager should look like. You need a stronger mentality to understand and analyze the world around you. You need to be strong emotionally to keep your head up when everyone around you makes you feel as if you are nothing. Your morals come into play. These are now on the top of your list. As the years go on, you will begin to question your morals. You might ask yourself what they mean to you or if you are serious and sincere in your beliefs. When determining what your morals are, keep in mind that your morals are your own. Some may contradict them, but they are yours and only yours.

Many pressures come along with being a teen. Right now you probably have it all planned out. You will say no to drugs, not have sex until you are married, and always keep your priorities straight. There is no such thing as a plan. Some of you will try smoking or drugs. Some of you will have sex. When the opportunity comes up, you will have other thoughts on your mind than everyone from your "childhood" telling you to "just say no!" Chances are you will be more concerned with what people around you are thinking. Trust me when I say, It's not hard to get addicted to things. I wish I had had the knowledge and sense to say no to certain things before they became a regular part of my life. I'm not proud of some things I do. I regret that these negative things have become a part of me and my identity.

It doesn't make you a bad person if you do decide to follow a certain path. It doesn't make you less of a person in God's eyes. The advice I want to give you isn't to tell you how to live your life. I just want you to be aware of consequences. There are consequences for all you do. If you have the knowledge of what could happen, maybe then you will rethink many things. It's okay to make mistakes, but only if you learn from them. One of the most important things you need to remember is that being a leader is more effective than being a follower.

Jillian

## I Had the Power

The transition from childhood to adolescence can be an exciting and difficult time in anyone's life. The safety and comforts of grade school and middle school virtually disappear. You are no longer ushered around school in a single-file line, and recess becomes but a pleasant memory. You are released into the freedom of high school, where you are not in control of the teachers but are at least in control of yourself. Your main focus turns from trying to get gold stars on your homework to trying to make the team, the play, or whatever else there is to get involved in. You are instilled with a new sense of power that your teachers, parents, and friends expect you not to abuse. It is up to you what you do with this power, but you must keep in mind the responsibility that comes along with it. For me this could not have been any more true.

As a child, you oftentimes talk with your friends about getting "crunked" and "scoring with all the * *," and you think that you are cool. This is just meaningless talk until you reach adolescence, when you find that your ignorant words become an alternative opportunity. Most everyone in high school knows somebody or at least knows somebody who knows somebody that does or sells drugs. Depending on if you have a part-time job or really generous parents, you find yourself with the resources to act on your childish talk. Nobody knows this better than my best friend.

All through grade school and middle school, we were as close as any friends could be. We hung out together, played on the same sports teams, and did all the other things that young boys do. This all changed however when we reached high school, and the path he chose to go down was one that I refused to follow. I was there to see his addiction start, and I had the power to prevent it. We were at Silver Dollar City enjoying the rides, or at least I was. When I looked into his eyes, I saw that something was missing. He was no longer his normal jovial self; he was a stranger. You see he had recently taken up smoking, and as I sat in the coaster with anticipation for the ride, he sat with a craving that he wanted to fix. I remember him escaping to the bathroom four times that day to satisfy his nicotine thirst, and with every cigarette a part of our friendship died. I had the opportunity to confront him about his problem but never the courage. I stood by and let him be taken over by a force much stronger then you or me. I had the power.

It only got worse from there. He moved on from cigarettes to alcohol to anything he could get his hands on. As he experimented with more and more drugs, I found myself getting farther and farther away. I talked with him several times about his problem, but I never made him hear me. I realize now that he needed me not to get farther away but to be closer than ever. I had the power to help him get caught, but instead I found myself helping him get away. I was the one who kept my mouth shut, I was the one who lied on his behalf, and I was the one who helped sneak him into his house so his parents would never know. I became his accomplice, and that is something I think about every time I look in his mother's eyes. I had the power.

We later decided to go our separate ways, and since then he has been busted a few times. His addiction is something he will continue to struggle with. Our once potent friendship has turned into nothing more then a nod of the head to acknowledge each other's presence. I had the power to prevent this from happening but never the audacity. I let myself down and above all I let my friend down. I encourage you not to let this happen to you or your friends. Do whatever it takes; make them listen. Have no regret, that is not what adolescence is about. I had the power, but now I am powerless.

[**Editor's note: Derogatory term for girls was omitted.]

*Patrick W. Kelly*

**It was a Friday night** about two weeks ago. My friend had a little party for his birthday, so I went. But when I arrived at his house, I really felt like going home. The reason was because I promised my mom and myself I wouldn't drink or do anything as dumb as that. But I was with my new high school friends, and I wanted to make a good impression, so I drank and, I guess to them, I did. But what I forgot was that I had a baseball game the next morning. I really wasn't being responsible because the next morning I couldn't even play because of how bad my stomach hurt. I really wish I could take that dumb decision back.

The reason I told you about my bad decision is because I wish somebody would have told me this when I was becoming a teenager. Not only did I let myself and my mom down, I let my whole team down. I really felt stupid, and I thought about what I had done simply to try to impress people. Now I am more experienced in decision making, so hopefully I am ready for the next big one.

Robert Aurilia

**Always be yourself** and don't be afraid to say no to anything you're even questionable about. I've learned that the hard way. You must have a lot of courage to be able to talk to one of your friends if they're doing something wrong. You might be taking the chance of them not talking to you for a while. It is worth it, believe me.

Kaylen Hyde

# Relating to Family

**I gained** my parents' trust by not lying to them and by doing what I was told. This is key to a relationship with parents. They have to trust their teen. When one receives their parents' trust, one has more freedom to have fun with friends. Sometimes it seems like I don't have to tell my parents everything, but the truth is, they care. My parents want me to be a part of their lives. Even though sometimes it might feel like it's a bore, I want my parents to be a part of my life as well.

Emily Gedert

**One of the things** I love about being a teen is the freedom that you get from your parents and guardians. With the freedom comes responsibility, but if you can show how responsible you are, you earn more freedom and leniency from your parents and guardians. This means you can hang out with your friends more often and longer, do more of the things you decide you want to do, and enjoy new adventures.

Colleen Glenn

## The Lost Son

My favorite Bible story is the parable of the lost son (Luke 14:11–32). I feel it offers encouragement for young people making the transition from childhood to adolescence. The lost son in the story represents the child facing his biggest challenges of becoming a teenager. The father in the parable represents the child's parents.

In the parable, the son goes to his father and asks for his share of the estate. That is like the child asking his parents for money to buy more expensive things. Children becoming teenagers today feel they need a cell phone, a computer, expensive clothes and sneakers, and money in their pockets to go to the movies or out to eat with their friends. Becoming a teenager is giving up your childhood games and toys and entering a new phase in your life. This new phase is difficult to deal with because there is peer pressure and other changes going on inside the child.

Sometimes parents act just like the father in the parable, by giving in to the demands of their children. Just like in the parable, the money didn't solve the son's problem, nor does it help the teenager's problem. Today kids get in all kinds of trouble with money, sometimes even drugs. The son in the parable spends all the money his father gives him. Teenagers today spend all the money their parents give them, and then they need and want more. In the parable, the son has a brother who gets jealous of how the father acts toward the son. I feel that when you become a teenager, your family puts more responsibilities on you. Your family expects you to always do the right thing. Just like the brother in the parable, there is always jealousy among siblings. One teenager thinks the other teenager or child in the family gets more than the other.

At the end of the parable, the father is so happy the lost son has returned home, even though the son did wrong. Just like in real life, most parents will accept their teenager's apology, when the teenager knows what he or she did wrong. Parents are real important when you are a teenager. Parents always love their children at any age, and forgive them. Parents' love is unconditional and forever; that is what makes their love so special.

It is so important to have religion in your life when you are a teenager. Just like the father in the parable, Jesus is always there to hear your problems and forgive you. Jesus has unconditional love for all his children of the Church. Teenagers sometimes stray from the Church. But all you have to remember is that Jesus is always there to take you back, whenever you decide to come back.

John Troino

**Some parents** really don't understand the world their teenagers are forced to live in. The times are different and very much evolved. Nowadays everyone has a computer in their home, kids as young as five have cell phones and fashion and music. Well, it's nothing like the 1960s and 70s.

But the basics of parenting are still the same. Moms and dads have the same reasons for not allowing you to do drugs now as their parents had when they were teenagers. Drugs are somewhat of an obvious no-no, but there are several other things parents often say, such as, "No! Because I said so!" and you just feel like you'll never know why. Parents say this because the reasoning behind their logic is too complicated for you to understand, and if they did try to explain it to you, you would just say it was stupid.

In the end, it's not parents that don't understand, its parents and kids that don't understand each other. They tried to get their parents to let them do the same stuff that we want to do, and their parents probably said no too. The kind of person we are and our safety are the most important things to our parents, whereas we are more concerned about our peers, our self-image, and how much fun we can have. We don't have a little person running around that was made from our flesh and bone to have to worry about and protect but, when we do, we will have to say the same things to them as our parents say to us. So, just remember, the next time mom or dad says, "Because I said so!" think of what it would be like to send a little piece of yourself that you carried, raised, and cherished out into a big scary world full of surprises and mishaps. Maybe then understanding each other won't be so difficult.

Claire Carson

**The relationship** with your family changes when you become a teenager. Your family will always be there for you no matter what, but you become less dependent on your parents, and you do a lot more things on your own. Your relationship with your siblings also changes. As I got older, my older brother and I became a lot closer. We hardly ever fight, and I know that I can talk with him about absolutely everything. My brother gives me helpful advice and never judges me.

Elena

## Nothing Better

Being a teenager is an exciting adventure. There is nothing better than turning sixteen, getting a set of car keys, and driving to meet your friends on a Friday night. When you become a teenager, parents begin to understand that you're growing up and capable of more responsibility, not too much, but enough to get your feet wet. The thrill of not having to depend on parents driving you everywhere is freeing. You feel so independent. The only thing you need to remember is to always be safe and listen to your parents, and if you do, your life will be a breeze.

Jessica Hoffman

## Always on Your Side

Becoming a teenager comes with many new responsibilities. Most children think that becoming a teenager is all about going to parties, being able to stay out later, and having parents who let you do more, but once you become a teenager, you actually get more responsibility put on you. Now I'm not saying that you still don't have fun, but your parents are going to monitor who you are hanging out with more closely and want to know where you are always going to be. Even if you are not trying to do the wrong thing or end up in the wrong place, sometimes unintentionally you may end up in a bad situation that you may not be able to handle. At these times, you need to be able to go to your parents. They are the people in your life who are always on your side, no matter what you may do. They will be able to help you figure out how to handle the situation in the correct manner. Although you may not want them to be the people you tell, they will be the ones who will be able to help you the most.

Victoria Roberts

**Growing up** I found myself saying things like, "I can't stand my little brother," or "I want new parents," when something didn't go my way. I can honestly say that sometimes I think that now. But I have realized that I wouldn't change my family for anything. No one is perfect. I think that forming a closer relationship with your parents is a key part of growing up. Think about it: when the world is against you, the only people who are there are your family.

Amber Bollinger

**When I was thirteen,** I felt invincible, and, of course, I knew everything. It was so annoying when my parents would tell me to "do my homework" or "go to bed." Who cared what I did or when I did it, as long as I kept doing well in school. I really didn't care about school because I wanted to have a life. You know what I mean, hanging out with friends, going to parties and the mall, and, of course, boys. That was what was important to me. Now that I'm seventeen, I regret my attitude and many of the things I did between the ages of thirteen and sixteen. I got emotionally hurt a number of times because I wanted to be in the popular group, so I said and did things that I'm not proud of. Over time, with the help of my family and faith community, I was able to get my priorities straight. I also feel horrible about what I put my parents through. All they ever showed me was love and support, and I gave them attitude and disrespect. So live your teenage years to the fullest, without going too far. You only have a short amount of time to enjoy the freedom of being a teenager. Just remember your parents are there to guide you.

Madeline Osbrink

**Friends come and go,** but family will always be there. Once you start high school, you become more independent and your relationships with your family change. You may be involved in more extracurricular activities, and you may not be home as often. Your parents will understand you're growing up. Always re-member to put family first, because they will always be there and love you no matter what.

Hope Emrisko

**When you become** a teenager, you may feel that school is getting harder and life is getting more complicated. You may also think that there is no one to turn to, but fear not because if you ever feel overwhelmed by this change in your life, you can always talk to your parents about whatever is troubling you. Now you may be thinking, "Yeah, my parents of all people, how can they possibly understand what I am going through, they probably don't even know what it's like being a teenager, right?" Wrong! Believe it or not, they were once young too, and they went through the same things you are going through now, and who knows, they may give you great advice that will help you out in the long run.

Kelle Landix

**As a teenager,** you tend to want to hang out with your friends more, leaving less time for your family. In our minds, we must always remember that we are not promised tomorrow. Living each day to the fullest and showing our loved ones how much they mean to us are what will make us truly happy no matter what age we are.

Nicole Marie Andrews

# Putting Media Messages in Perspective

**Your teen years** are when you get to discover who you really are as a person, but discovering the true you isn't very easy. It is hard to find the real you because of the media today. The media tell teens that we have to dress, talk, and act a certain way to be accepted as one of the cool kids. Keep in mind what is important to you and what goals you would like to accomplish in life.

*Brittany*

**The media** have done more to negatively harm the image of teenagers than any other institution. In the media, teenagers are portrayed as materialistic, lustful, deceitful, petty, and vain. The reality could not be further from this image. In actuality, teenagers care about their community and peers. Instead of reinforcing the positive achievements of teenagers, the media focus only on our faults. Other teenagers, wishing to fulfill the media's image, do foolish and individualistic things that they might not have otherwise done.

*Dane Davis*

## What the Media Have Taught Me

As I was flipping through a magazine, I couldn't help but notice that every girl was the same. They were all perfect! No zits, freckles, or imperfections of any kind. As I was looking at one of the many perfume ads, I was appalled that the model was hardly wearing anything and was thrown across a guy without his shirt on. Let's face it, we all know that if we really go and buy that perfume, that's not really going to happen. Every ad, no matter what they were selling, had a sexual picture. Every girl by a pool was wearing a bikini. Every girl in a prom dress was showing her cleavage and had the perfect date. Every girl in school had her hair done perfectly and was wearing the most perfect outfit and had all the guys smiling around her. Those girls aren't real. Every girl can't fit into a bikini or have the perfect hair with the perfect outfit and the perfect guy. It took me many years and many magazines to figure out that no girl is absolutely perfect. Everyone has flaws, so people just have them Photoshopped out. It is important to wake up in the morning and look in the mirror and tell yourself that you are beautiful. You may not be perfect, and there may be a new zit on your face, but that's okay because if you look around at school, you will realize that everyone else is going through the same changes you are. It is important that when you read magazines, you remember that everyone is beautiful and unique in their own individual way.

Alysa Shupe

## Beauty

Every time one turns on the television, looks through magazines, or passes billboards on the highway, the advertising is all about beautiful, skinny, or muscular-looking men and women. The images draw all eyes to stare, making one wish he or she could look like that. Well, here's a news flash. Ordinary people do not look like that; they look the way God made them, and not how the media, surgery, or makeup can make them look. These images of beautiful people are affecting young children today and giving them the wrong idea of beauty.

Teen magazines and news reports are full of stories or articles about how someone suffers from an eating disorder, or went through some kind of surgery, because they did not like the way they looked. Every time I see this, I become angrier with the media and the pop stars. They are putting such a negative picture in young peoples' minds. This causes them to think they are ugly and makes them want to change how they look. I just wish people would see that each and every one of us is unique in our own way and that is how God wanted us to be. If he wanted us all to look the same, then he would have done so, but instead, he made each one of us different, and we need to appreciate that.

I think that all men, women, and children need to discover how beautiful they really are no matter how skinny or fat, buff, or fit they are. Each one of us is beautiful in God's eyes, and we need to see it in our own eyes. If we do, we can love ourselves for who we are. I have come to discover that the people I call my friends love me for who I am inside and not what is on the outside. They do not judge me by my looks or appearance. They look past that and see the beauty that is within me.

Valerie Waugh

**Skinny girls,** name-brand materials, nice hair, rich lifestyles, and the latest technology. Today the media have their own model of how they want us to be. Their target is innocent, developing teens that will go after the bait. Just think about it. What was on the cover of the last magazine you picked up? How was the model portrayed? Then again, what about the latest commercial you saw? What about the latest reality show on television? It's funny, but they all most likely had something in common. They probably had a model that was so skinny that she looked anorexic. They might have been advertising new hair products or name-brand clothing. This is the media saying, "This is how I want you to be and this is the only way you'll be accepted." I'm sorry, but even though it seems to be, a luxurious lifestyle and the "cool" way to be, it's quite empty. Teens portrayed in movies smoking, drinking, and partying hard isn't what I would exactly call "healthy" or the "good life."

Growing teens, during their time of maturation, absorb their surroundings. In a society like ours, many teens who are not sure of themselves or have a low self-esteem succumb to the messages about ideals conveyed by the media. Life isn't about being materialistic. It obviously isn't what God calls us to be. The pressure to be like the images portrayed by the media is so great that it drives people to desperate measures. For example, dieting in order to get the perfect body, just like the ones of the models that appear on the latest *Seventeen* or *Cosmo Girl* magazines, has driven some girls to endanger their lives with anorexia. Is this what God calls us to do—endanger our lives in order to fit in and be accepted by others? No, it's not, in fact God doesn't care about how nice or perfect we look or what new objects we have, but rather about how we are on the inside. God made us all unique. We all have our own physical features that no one else can match up to. God loves us for who we are and wants us to be happy with what he gave us. If we go around accepting what the media offer, without actually saying it, we are rejecting God's calling for us. All of the luxury, clothing, and perfect bodies are just the frosting on the cake. What counts is what is inside of us. What is really inside the cake counts. Do we really want to be that superficial? No! Following the media's message is not what God is calling us to do or be.

Barbara Cáceres

**The media show** us images of these skinny, young, pretty movie stars: the ideal person. Well, with the exception of a few genetically inclined people, nobody really looks like that. Images from television and magazines put too much pressure on teenagers to have the perfect body, hair, face, and everything. It's causing some people to take drastic efforts to look like them. Anorexia and bulimia are two big ways that many girls change the way they appear. But is this how God intended for your life to go? Absolutely not! God created you a specific way because that's what he wanted.

The most important thing to remember is to just appreciate you for yourself. Now you're probably saying, "Oh, what's she talking about? She has no idea about any of this." Well, actually I do. I'll be the first to admit that I'm not a very skinny person; my thighs are too big, my stomach has chub, I have what I'd like to call "passion handles" (no, not just love handles). For a long time, I was very self-conscious about how I looked and dressed and acted, until one day I heard this speech that a boy gave. In it he mentioned that those who wish they were different waste their whole lives trying to get there; instead, you should turn your attention to what your good attributes are. I can perform on stage, some people can play sports, and other people are good at working with children. There are hundreds of things you can think of. The important thing is to find you and just be you.

Olivia Gjurich

# Using Technology

**Technology** is the driving force in our society. The amount of change we have experienced as young adults has never been seen before in the history of humankind. New technological inventions have made the world more efficient, enjoyable, and easy. Nevertheless, these new inventions can and do separate families and friends from our lives. The allure of video games, the Internet, or an MP3 player is hard to overcome by many teenagers. Teenagers must remember that for every moment they spend with a machine, they are spending one less moment with those who truly love them. Technology must be embraced, but it must also be used with caution.

Dane Davis

**You have to be careful** when using technology. Even these new video games that have online gaming can allow a person to trick you into meeting him or her. Be smart with your computer, your cell phone, and even your video games because you never know when someone is fooling you or lying about who he or she really is.

James Cannon

**My experience** with technology today has been good. I have a lot of it. I use the Internet, cell phone, Xbox, Xbox360, PlayStation 2, PSP, Camera, and AOL Instant Messenger, etc. They all can serve a good purpose.

The Internet is good and bad. It is an excellent resource for reports, finding facts, and talking to people you know and love. If you don't see a friend anymore because you don't have time or you go to a different school, then you can use Instant Messenger to keep in touch. I do this with my friends that I don't see often that go to other schools. The Internet can also be a dangerous place. It is filled with junk mail, viruses, spam, and predators, if you go to chat rooms. I don't go to those places. I wouldn't recommend other young people going there either. You hear way too many stories of kids getting hurt this way. Yes, use the Internet, but don't give out your information, stay out of chat rooms, and only talk to people you know.

A cell phone is another good source of technology. You can talk to a friend to find out where you are meeting. It is a good way to keep in touch with your parents so they know where you are and that you're okay. It is also good in case of an emergency, like if you get into a car accident, you can call someone, or during a blackout, you can call someone else's phone to communicate. But don't go crazy with it. Don't go over your minutes. It is very easy to run up a high phone bill.

Xbox 360, Xbox, Playstation 2, and PSP are some of the great video games. They are entertaining when you are bored and have nothing to do. If no one is home or available to hang out with, you can play video games to pass the time. There are a variety of games with great story lines. Some are almost like reading a book. Just don't let these things distract you from doing your schoolwork. Don't let them distract you from anything else important or any responsibilities you may have. Video games can relieve stress from school or if you are having a bad day. Just don't forget it's just a game.

Remember, technology is good as long as you don't use it in the wrong way.

Frank Mormando

**As you may have seen** on the news, the MySpace Web site has become very popular among teenagers. Whether you have a profile on MySpace or you know someone who does, I would like to take some time and inform you about some of the dangers of opening yourself up to the cyberworld. I'm sure that you have seen the news about young people being contacted and tracked down by online predators. I had a profile on MySpace, but when my parents saw all the news that was coming out about this Web site, they decided to block the Web site on my computer. At first I was mad because the only reason I had a profile was to talk to my friends. My parents did not care how much I pleaded to keep my profile and, to this day, I am still not allowed to go on the Web site. Even if you are like me and in denial, saying that nothing bad could ever happen to you, you have to face reality and look at all the signs. I began to see why people were getting so worked up about this Web site.

If you have a profile on MySpace, I would like to give you a little advice. Make sure you know everyone on your friends list. Don't talk to someone you don't recognize, even if they say that they know you. I also suggest that you don't put any pictures on MySpace, but if you really want pictures, then put group pictures on so that the person who views your profile doesn't totally know what you look like.

Megan Walkowiak

**Watching television** and playing with electronics is not bad, but remember to stay healthy and enjoy other activities and workouts. Other than that, we are on the edge of a new era in technology, and I can't wait to witness it.

Rocky Salemmo

**There are many times** when talking on the Internet is extremely fun, especially when it's with your friends. Although you may think the Internet is just fun, it can also be dangerous.

When you enter chat rooms on the Internet and start talking to people you don't know, it's kind of scary. Believe it or not, you truly have no idea who may be trying to track you down. There are a lot of weird people out there who are trying to pump information from people to find out where they live. That just isn't right. If you give them personal information, it could lead to some very bad things happening. Say there is a person you have been talking to on the Internet for a while whom you think you know, but truly you're wrong. You don't know them at all. They may be lying to you about their age, and trying to make you comfortable enough to tell them things, such as where you live, your phone number, how old you are, etc. You should never even think twice about answering those questions. That is none of their business, and they don't need to know that. Even if you don't give personal information to people, they still may be able to find it out. Some people sit and wait for the right person to target, which is really scary. They can track you down by using their computer, and they can find out any information about you including where you live. If you are talking in these chat rooms, you have no idea who could show up at your house one day. This is exactly why you shouldn't talk to strangers on the Internet.

Amanda Dupont

**We all use** a variety of types of technology, but sometimes people use it for not so good reasons. In today's world, we have all sorts of technology that we can use for communication: cell phones, phones, text messaging, and even computers. Some people think that it is cool to talk to the young people of the world on these devices and then end up hurting them.

Many of us teens use AOL, instant messaging, MySpace, and other communication devices to talk to our friends or any other person who will talk to us. But you should really only talk to people you know and only when you know it is truly that person. When some really cute older person talks to us, it makes us feel cool and like we are totally grown up and can do whatever we want. We know that it is wrong, but we love that feeling we get when we talk to that person. We hear the stories on the news, on television shows, movies, and even from our parents and friends, but we never think that it could actually happen to us. The truth is that it can. The person you are talking to online will say anything to make you trust him or her and then will start talking to you all the time and make you feel wanted. You will start to think that you totally know that person and that you have a relationship with him or her. If you believe that, then you are just falling for the same act that many teenagers and preteens have fallen for before. What I am trying to say is that you should listen to your parents and think twice before you use MySpace, AOL, e-mail, or instant messaging to meet new people and before you put your picture online. Stick to meeting people the old-fashioned way and you won't end up hurting your future or hurting yourself.

*Kaitlyn Valls*

## Electronics Are Running My Life

The technology industry today is bigger than ever. Everywhere I turn, I see someone talking on their cell phone, listening to their iPod, or text messaging friends. For us as high school students, these new technologies are our biggest distractions.

During my freshman year, I was completely wrapped up in the bliss of Instant Messenger. Every day after school, I was on it until eleven o'clock at night. This caused a problem when it came to homework. I would have to be up until midnight or one finishing it for the next day.

When I was a sophomore, I became extremely busy. I was in the musical in the fall, speech team in the winter, and track and field in the spring. This made it extremely difficult for me to be on IM all the time and still make time for homework. I think that was my first reality check. Obviously, it was hard to put my schoolwork over my friends, but in the end, that was the best decision. Instead of talking to them for hours on end every night, I would only talk to them for an hour maybe three times a week.

This year, my junior year, my friends have become just as busy as I am, which actually worked out. Now we all have reasons for not being able to talk to one another, and we all have something to do instead of talking to one another all the time. We still keep in touch, and it's good to know that we can go for a week not talking to one another and still be good friends. My advice to you is as long as you learn to budget your time, you will have plenty of time for both friends and schoolwork.

Michele Onwochei

**When I** was in eighth grade, my dad bought me a cell phone. I can still remember the day I got it. I walked into cheerleading practice thinking I was so cool. And the first time I got a screen name on AOL, I was so excited because I thought that at that time I was really becoming a teenager. Now that everyone has these things, we look at them as necessities. What would we do without our cell phones, our text messaging, and our instant messaging? I know that I would be lost in a way. I try to remember not to take these things for granted. Seriously, we don't realize what it takes for us to have cell phones and computers. We all need to realize these are just material things. We shouldn't get into fights with our parents about not having the latest things.

Amber Bollinger

*Using Technology*

# Acknowledgments

The scriptural quotation on page 52 is from the New American Bible with Revised New Testament and Revised Psalms. Copyright © 1991, 1985, and 1970 by the Confraternity of Christian Doctrine, Washington, DC. Used by the permission of the copyright owner. All rights reserved. No part of the New American Bible may be reproduced in any form without permission in writing from the copyright owner.

The "Prayer of Serenity" on page 52 is by Reinhold Niebuhr.

The prayer by Mother Teresa on page 57 was found at *www.elise.com/quotes/a/mother_teresa_people_are_often_unreasonable.php,* accessed October 9, 2006.

To view copyright terms and conditions for Internet materials cited here, log on to the home pages for the referenced Web sites.

During this book's preparation, all citations, facts, figures, names, addresses, telephone numbers, Internet URLs, and other pieces of information cited within were verified for accuracy. The authors and Saint Mary's Press staff have made every attempt to reference current and valid sources, but we cannot guarantee the content of any source, and we are not responsible for any changes that may have occurred since our verification. If you find an error in, or have a question or concern about, any of the information or sources listed within, please contact Saint Mary's Press.

**"I like the advice.** It will help me in my future as a teenager."

Cassidy Bittle

**"This book tells me** to never give up and to have faith in myself."

Drew Fakler

**"I recommend this to other kids.** It is a collection of advice about growing up. At school if you don't fit in a group, keep trying until you find the right one."

Colin